CONSTRUCTING A SAINT
THROUGH IMAGES

The 1609 Illustrated Biography of Ignatius of Loyola

CONSTRUCTING A SAINT
THROUGH IMAGES

The 1609 Illustrated Biography of Ignatius of Loyola

INTRODUCTORY ESSAY BY

John W. O'Malley, S.J.

LATIN CAPTIONS TRANSLATED BY

James P. M. Walsh, S.J.

SAINT JOSEPH'S UNIVERSITY PRESS
PHILADELPHIA

Library of Congress Cataloging-in-Publication Data

Vita beati patris Ignatii Loiolae. English.
    Constructing a saint through images : the 1609 illustrated biography of Ignatius of
Loyola / introductory essay by John W. O'Malley ; Latin captions translated by James
P.M. Walsh.
        p. cm.
    ISBN-13: 978-0-916101-58-9 (hardcover : alk. paper)
    ISBN-10: 0-916101-58-4 (hardcover : alk. paper)
  1. Ignatius, of Loyola, Saint, 1491-1556. 2. Ignatius, of Loyola, Saint, 1491-1556–Art.
3. Christian saints–Spain–Biography. I. O'Malley, John W. II. Walsh, James P. M.
III. Title.
  BX4700.L7V5813 2008
  271'.5302–dc22
  [B]
  2008037601

Saint Joseph's University Press
5600 City Avenue
Philadelphia, PA 19131
www.sjupress.com

Cover design: Jonathan Dart
Book design and typesetting: Carol McLaughlin

Saint Joseph's University Press is a member of the Association of Jesuit University Presses.

CONTENTS

PREFACE

Constructing a Saint through Images is an annotated facsimile reproduction of an illustrated life of Ignatius of Loyola published in Rome in 1609 to celebrate his beatification that year by Pope Paul V. That original edition was also meant to foster Ignatius' cult and to promote the cause for his canonization as a saint, which occurred thirteen years later, 1622. The book is important, therefore, for the reasons it was originally published, as well as for the influence it had on subsequent Jesuit iconography. It is, however, especially important because of the exquisite quality of its eighty-one copperplate engravings. The engraver was Jean-Baptiste Barbé, and one of the artists involved in the project was almost certainly Peter Paul Rubens.

Next year, 2009, is the four-hundredth anniversary of the publication of the *Vita beati patris Ignatii Loiolae.* To honor the occasion and to make the book more widely available, Saint Joseph's University Press has published this annotated facsimile edition. Aside from Latin captions describing the scenes depicted, the *Vita* was without text. In our edition James P. M. Walsh's translations of the Latin captions appear on the left-hand pages, facing the images. At the foot of those pages I indicate literary sources upon which the scenes depicted in the images were based. The pages were blank in the original. The images themselves are here reproduced at 100% of their original size.

In my introduction I identify the people involved in producing the *Vita*, analyze early biographies of Ignatius leading up to it, and describe the special features of the *Vita.* I also indicate how the Jesuits used print and image to promote Ignatius' beatification and canonization. To help readers unfamiliar with Ignatius' life, a chronology of it is here included on page 35.

I am grateful to Joseph A. Haller, S.J., curator *emeritus* of university fine print collections at Georgetown University, for calling the anniversary to my attention. Carmen Croce and Joseph Chorpenning, directors of Saint Joseph's University Press, have guided this project from beginning to end with their customary energy, imagination, and commitment to excellence in book publication. They and I are grateful to Jill Thomas, curator of the Jesuitana collection of the Burns Library of Boston College, for her counsel and for providing the image on page 2.

John W. O'Malley, S.J.

The Many Lives of Ignatius of Loyola
Future Saint

In 1609 Ignatius of Loyola was declared "blessed," the preliminary step to canonization. To celebrate the event, the Jesuits that year published the *Vita beati patris Ignatii Loiolae.* They republished it in 1622, the year Ignatius was canonized, adding to it another engraving depicting the ceremony (Figure 1). The road to Ignatius' beatification and canonization had been long and difficult, but by 1609 one goal had been achieved and the other was within sight. The Jesuits hoped the *Vita* would inspire popular devotion to Ignatius and move forward the process of his canonization.

The *Vita* was certainly not the first illustrated saint's life—or, in this case, future saint's life. In Rome in 1584, for instance, there appeared a life of Saint Francis of Paola illustrated with thirty-eight engravings by Ambrosius Brambilla.[1] In 1603 there appeared in Antwerp a life of Saint Catherine of Siena engraved by Philips Galle,[2] and around the same time a life of John the Baptist engraved by Jacques de Weert was published there that consisted in a a title-page and twenty-one plates.[3] In 1608, the year before the publication of the *Vita*, there appeared in Rome a life of Saint Francis of Assisi designed and engraved by Philippe Thomassin, which consisted in a title-page and fifty-one plates.[4] The *Vita Ignatii* of 1609 with its eighty-one copper plate engravings— seventy-nine biographical scenes, plus title-page and frontispiece—took its place in this young genre as its most elaborate exemplar.

The *Vita*, whose production was encouraged by Claudio Aquaviva, the superior general of the Society of Jesus, was just one element in the Jesuits' strategy for making Ignatius known and for showing how his holiness fit the pattern of the saints who preceded him. Planning for it got underway in 1605-06. Pope Paul V, elected in 1605, had that very year allowed the process for Ignatius' beatification/canonization to begin, the first concrete indication that the Jesuits' hopes for their founder might be fulfilled. Paul's action gave impetus to the decision to produce the *Vita*. Although first published on the occasion of the beatification, it was from the beginning ultimately directed to the crowning step—the canonization engraving published in 1622 was already in proofs at the same time as those for the engravings published in 1609.[5]

The book was characteristically Jesuit in that it was a collaborative effort on an international scale. Of the two Jesuits who in Rome principally coordinated the

Sollenni Catholicæ Ecclesiæ ritu, ac ceremonia in Sanctoru̅ numerum á GREGORIO XV. *Pont.Max.refertur. Die* XII *Martij Anno* MD C XXII .

Figure 1. Jean-Baptiste Barbé and Peter Paul Rubens (?).
Engraving 80, *The Canonization Ceremony,* in *Vita beati patris Ignatii Loiolae,* 1622 edition.
Used with permission of the John J. Burns Library, Boston College.
Caption: By the customary rite and ceremony of the Catholic Church, he is enrolled among the saints by the Supreme Pontiff Gregory XV, on the twelfth day of March in the year 1622.

project, one was a Pole, Nicolas Lancicius (Mikołaj Lęczycki) and the other an Italian, Filippo Rinaldi. Nothing is known about Rinaldi except that at the time he worked on the *Vita*, he was rector of the German College in Rome. About Lancicius, however, who most likely composed the captions, we know a great deal.

He was born in 1574 in the Polish-Lithuanian Commonwealth near Vilnius, and at an early age converted to Catholicism from Calvinism. He entered the Jesuits in Cracow in 1592 and was sent almost immediately to Rome for his training. Beginning in 1601, he assisted Niccolò Orlandini in his important *Historia Societatis Iesu*. Orlandini died in 1606, having finished only the *pars prima, sive Ignatius*, which was a year-by-year account of the history of the Society of Jesus from 1540, the year the order was founded, until 1556, the year Ignatius died. In 1603, Francesco Sacchini also began helping Orlandini, after whose death he revised the manuscript and brought it to publication finally in 1614.[6]

Lancicius was therefore well qualified for undertaking the *Vita*. He later held responsible positions in the Society. He was, for instance, rector of the Jesuit college in Cracow, 1621-31, and provincial superior of the Lithuanian Province, 1631-35. Besides other writings of ascetical and devotional nature, he left behind a small corpus of occasional pieces about Ignatius. In 1622, on the occasion of Ignatius' canonization, he published in Cracow, anonymously, a small work entitled *Gloria S. Ignatii*, which was several times reprinted.[7]

Even more important in the production of the book were, of course, the artists and the engraver Rinaldi and Lancicius enlisted. Ursula König-Nordhoff, who has studied the *Vita* in meticulous detail, has convincingly argued that all the work on the book was done in Rome. The Roman provenance strengthens the thesis that the young Peter Paul Rubens, who arrived in Rome in late 1605, was involved in the project. Jean-Baptiste Barbé, another Fleming who was in Rome at the time, was the chief designer of most or all of the images. He consulted a number of visual sources and then revised or adapted drawings he had solicited from a small group of masters.[8]

Barbé, born in Antwerp in 1578, was a disciple of the noted engraver Philips Galle.[9] As a young man, he spent some years in Rome, where he came to the attention of Rinaldi and Lancicius. While in Rome, he met Rubens and produced with him a beautiful engraving of the Holy Family.[10] Shortly after the publication of the *Vita* he returned to Antwerp, where he married the daughter of Hieronymus Wierix, who was a member of the team that produced for the Jesuits the magnificent 153 engravings of the *Annotationes et meditationes in evangelia*, first published in 1595 and based on the text of Jerónimo Nadal, the peripatetic agent-in-the-field of Saint Ignatius.[11] Wierix was also the engraver for a twelve-plate depiction of miracles and supernal interventions in Ignatius' life, published in Antwerp at an unknown date but probably before 1609.[12]

Barbé was thus firmly incorporated into the brilliant network of Antwerp engravers and into the Jesuits' relationship to it.

Rubens' name has long been associated with the *Vita*. König-Nordhoff, while showing the problems that tradition entails, nonetheless concludes that Rubens is a likely candidate for the drawings Barbé turned into the best engravings.[13] It is certain, moreover, that Rubens during his Roman sojourn began his association with the Jesuits that he would continue on close terms for the rest of his life. In 1605, for instance, he executed a Circumcision of Christ for the high altar of the Jesuit church in Genoa. A few years later, he created for the Jesuits a pair of oil paintings representing Ignatius and Francis Xavier, with the former clad not in a simple cassock but in a chasuble, that is, in a vestment that specified him as a priest (Figures 2 and 3). This is the first painting in which Ignatius was thus depicted, a half-century after his death.[14]

This pair, and Rubens' later versions of it, set a standard for Jesuit iconography of the two saints from this time forward. It promoted the practice in Jesuit churches around the world of dedicating an altar to Ignatius to the left of the main altar and one to Xavier to the right. In Antwerp Rubens produced for the Jesuits' new church an astounding cycle of paintings, which unfortunately were later destroyed by fire.[15] His association with the Jesuits was not simply professional: at their church in Antwerp he was an active member of the Marian Congregation or Sodality of Our Lady, the Jesuits equivalent of a lay confraternity.

Thus the *Vita* is important for several reasons—the number and exquisite quality of the engravings, the role Rubens almost certainly played in the undertaking, the occasion for which it was produced, the influence it had on subsequent Jesuit iconography, and the place in holds in the Jesuit campaign for Ignatius' canonization. Because of the many copies that survive, we can infer that the book had a large print-run. For what audience was it intended? Since the book was published not only without indication of author or publisher but also without a preface, the question can be answered only by inference. A parent or catechist who knew the general outline of Ignatius' life could certainly have used the *Vita* to instruct and inspire children, but the authors obviously aimed much higher. The quality of the engravings and the sophisticated Latin of the captions point to an adult, refined, and well-educated public.

The Early Accounts

The history leading up to the *Vita* begins some seventy-five years earlier at the University of Paris. There, in the early 1530s, Ignatius and nine other students decided to travel together to the Holy Land to live at least for a while

Figure 2. Peter Paul Rubens, *St. Ignatius of Loyola*, c. 1608.
Oil on canvas. 88.2 x 53.1 inches.
Samuel von Brukenthal Collection, inv. 995.
The National Brukenthal Museum, Sibiu, Romania.

6

Figure 3. Peter Paul Rubens, *St. Francis Xavier*, c. 1608.
Oil on canvas. 88.6 x 53.1 inches.
Samuel von Brukenthal Collection, inv. 996.
The National Brukenthal Museum, Sibiu, Romania.

where Jesus lived and, presumably, to work there for the conversion of the Muslims. Among these ten was Francis Xavier, the famous future missionary to the Far East.

By 1537 they had all gathered in Venice to await passage, but because of the treacherous political situation in the Mediterranean, they were unable to accomplish their goal. Two years later they were in Rome, where they decided to stay together for good and to form a new religious order. They were already calling their group "the brotherhood of Jesus" (*Compagnia di Gesù*), and they agreed to keep that name, should their new order be approved. Its Latin form was *Societas Iesu.* On September 27, 1540, Pope Paul III approved the order, making it a formally recognized institution within the Catholic church.

The papal bull listed as founding members the ten former students, by now priests, but, significantly, it listed Ignatius first. Although at this stage these "friends in the Lord," as they referred to themselves, were technically equals, they recognized that it was Ignatius who had brought them together, had led most of them through his *Spiritual Exercises,* and was the almost inevitable choice for superior general. Sure enough, on April 19 the following year, they elected Ignatius by a unanimous vote except for Ignatius' own. They could not have done better. They rightly revered him for his spiritual and religious gifts, but they also saw in him a leader who could guide the order with an unusual combination of prudence and boldness.

Ignatius, fifty years old when elected, set about his task with vigor, which he needed for holding together the rapidly expanding Society that numbered about a thousand members by the time he died fifteen years later. The Society attracted to itself men of extraordinary talent, such as Francisco de Borja (Borgia), the former Duke of Gandia, and Peter Canisius, the person singly most responsible for rallying German Catholics in the second part of the century. Although men like these help explain the success of Ignatius' generalship, they did not regularly reside in Rome so as to have a hand in the central government of the order.

Ignatius nowhere showed his gifts of leadership more brilliantly than in his choice of two men to aid him directly in that task. The first was Juan Alfonso de Polanco, a talented and well-educated Spanish priest from a wealthy, "New Christian" family of Burgos, who joined the order the year after it was founded. Six years later Ignatius named him secretary, a post he continued to fill for the next two generals. The second was the Majorcan, Jerónimo Nadal, who entered in 1545. He became Ignatius' agent in the field, traveling throughout Europe explaining to members what it meant to be a Jesuit and then reporting back to headquarters. These three together formed a powerful team, which eclipsed the influence of the original companions of Paris. This phenomenon led to the growing persuasion inside and outside the order that Ignatius alone was the founder, just as Saints Dominic and Francis had been founders of theirs.

Polanco had hardly become secretary of the Society when in 1547 he asked Diego Laínez to write an account "for our edification" of how the order came to be. Laínez, one of the original band, did as requested.[16] His text seems to have had fairly wide circulation in manuscript among Jesuits. The next year Polanco complemented Laínez' narrative with information he received from elsewhere and composed a longer "summary" of the basic story.[17] From the beginning, therefore, the Jesuits showed a concern for the history of their order, at the center of whose origins was Ignatius.[18]

Both Laínez and Polanco devoted the first part of their accounts exclusively to the life of Ignatius up to his arrival at Paris, after which he became the major figure in a larger story. They both open their narratives with Ignatius' wounding in the battle of Pamplona, 1521, the point at which his spiritual conversion began. Laínez ends his account about the time of the founding, 1540, but Polanco goes a little longer. Both of them knew a great deal about Ignatius' life from Pamplona forward, most of which had to come directly or indirectly from Ignatius himself. In their accounts they presented him as a man of singular holiness. According to them, Ignatius received from God extraordinary illuminations about the mysteries of the Christian faith and on occasion he was able to foresee future events; his prayers were powerful with God for the healing of the sick. Neither Laínez nor Polanco, however, mentions any visions of Christ or the saints, which would play such a big role in the account of his life Ignatius subsequently dictated to Luis Gonçalves da Câmara.

Polanco, many years later, in 1574, after he had been relieved of his position as secretary, returned to the subject. Whereas in his "summary" of 1548 he was more concerned with the origins of the Society than with a proper biography of Ignatius, he now professedly wrote a *vita*. At that time he had at his disposal the biography of Ignatius published in Latin by Pedro de Ribadeneyra two years earlier, to say nothing of the account from Ignatius himself, the "autobiography." Although Polanco's *vita* repeated some of the errors from his "summary," it added important information that he gathered from his long and particularly close association with Ignatius.[19] This time, moreover, Polanco recounts Ignatius' visions of Christ and the saints.[20]

The Jesuits were almost indefatigable writers of memoranda and letters, and in them during the first two generations of the order, they often touched on matters relating to Ignatius and the earliest years of the order. In the twentieth century, such materials were collected and published as the *Fontes narrativi* in the series *Monumenta Historica Societatis Iesu*. They fill four large volumes, three of which run to over 800 pages. Jesuits' interest in origins was more than a nostalgic glance backwards. The Society, while in a general way conforming to the patterns of religious life established by the mendicant orders of the thirteenth century like the Dominicans and Franciscans, had features that were distinctive. How to convey those features to recruits to the order in places where they had no chance of meeting Loyola or any of the other "founders"? How to establish a corporate identity and make it credible and transmissible? How to defend the order against those who attacked it as a betrayal of the traditions of religious life?[21] The Jesuits had no body of literature to call their own that they could hand to friends, enemies, or potential recruits to explain who they were and what they were about. Accounts of how they came to be could help remedy the situation.

What was missing was an account directly from Ignatius, who resisted efforts to provide it. His reticence is surprising because earlier he seems to have spoken rather freely about his life, as the narratives by Laínez and Polanco indicate. Polanco and especially Nadal tried to persuade him.[22] What they wanted was more than a simple chronicle. They wanted him to give them an account of how God had guided him from the time of his spiritual conversion until the present. The work would be a "testament" for members of the Society. As motivation, they told Ignatius that founders of other religious orders had bequeathed such documents to their followers and that it behooved Ignatius to do the same. They probably had in mind Francis of Assisi's "Testament," which more than suggests they were already equating Ignatius with saintly founders.

Nadal broached the matter to Ignatius in 1551. Ignatius brushed him off, saying that he had neither the inclination nor the time for it. The next year, after Nadal returned to Rome from Sicily, he asked him again, and did the same when he returned much later from a long sojourn in Spain. Ignatius finally acquiesced and, toward the end of August 1553, began dictating his story to a young Portuguese Jesuit Luis Gonçalves da Câmara.[23] Ignatius interrupted his narration after a few weeks and did not resume it until seventeen months later, on March 9, 1555. After another few weeks, he again interrupted it and did not bring it to conclusion until the autumn.

This account, sometimes called Ignatius' autobiography, is in fact without title. Nadal called it simply "The Acts of Father Ignatius," *Acta*. Ignatius throughout his narrative refers to himself in the third person as "the pilgrim," and therefore the work is sometimes called "the pilgrim's story." It begins only in 1521 with the battle of Pamplona, which, as mentioned, is where Laínez and Polanco begin their accounts. This has to be the point where Ignatius habitually began to talk about his life. He would have been about thirty years old at the time of the battle, which leaves many years unaccounted for.

The *Acta* abounds in critical problems. Gonçalves da Câmara listened as Ignatius dictated. He then went to his room and jotted down some notes. Some time later—days or weeks?—he elaborated upon the notes and for the first two segments dictated the results to a Spanish scribe. He dictated the last segment, from the fall of 1555, to an Italian scribe, which means that segment was in Italian. Though credited with a superb memory, he surely has not transmitted to posterity a verbatim. Moreover, Ignatius, a Spaniard, told his story to a Portuguese auditor, who in turn dictated the results of his notes first to a Spaniard, and then to an Italian. Many steps intervened, therefore, between what Ignatius actually said and what ended up on paper. More basically, the account suffers from all the problems endemic to a personal memoir, in which the author self-selects from events that happened decades earlier. In this case, furthermore, Ignatius spoke from memory without referring to notes or documentation.

The final product was translated into Latin by a French Jesuit, Annibal du Coudret, sometime between 1559 and 1561. Although never printed, the document circulated in manuscript among members of the Society until 1567. Pedro de Ribadeneyra, who wrote the first published biography of Ignatius and who knew Ignatius extremely well, criticized the *Acta* for inaccuracies, alleging that at times Gonçalves da Câmara's memory failed him.[24] Ribadeneyra granted, however, that in essentials "the pilgrim's story," as we have it, was reliable. The basic story-line can for the most part be corroborated by other sources already mentioned, as well as by a much later recollection of what happened in the 1530s from another of the original band, Simâo Rodrigues.[25] The result was that even before Ignatius died the Jesuits had considerable biographical information on a major part of his life.

Ignatius brought his *Acta* up only to 1538, the year before he and the other nine companions of Paris decided to form a religious order. He lived until 1556, the year after he finished dictating his story. That leaves eighteen more years unaccounted for, during fifteen of which he was the superior general. As Ignatius tells his story in the *Acta* he does not point it toward the founding. The story is "the story of a soul," that is, the story of his relationship with God and, more particularly, how God guided him from a superficial grasp of what the relationship entailed to something far deeper. It is a story that includes depression, internal illuminations, supernatural visions, and suspicions about his orthodoxy on the part of ecclesiastical authorities, who in every instance eventually declared him innocent. It is the story of a man who was during these years a sometimes soldier, then in succession an ascetical solitary, a mendicant pilgrim, a mid-life university student, and, finally, an itinerant preacher. After those careers, he became the chief executive officer of a nascent world-wide organization. By the time he died, Jesuits were present in every country in Western Europe, as well as in Brazil, India, and Japan.

The foundational importance of the *Acta* is corroborated by how faithfully the first part of the *Vita* of 1609 follows it. The *Vita* nonetheless tampers with the story in one important way. It tells of miracles Ignatius worked during this period of his life, which are altogether absent in the original story, and it sometimes otherwise embellishes what we find in Ignatius' account. A half-century had intervened, during which the Jesuits shaped and reshaped their founder's life to adapt it to the different audiences they hoped to reach, not least of which, especially by about 1588, was the Congregation of Rites and the pope himself.

Meanwhile, Nadal had seized upon the pilgrim's story as the basis for many of his exhortations to Jesuit communities throughout Europe, using it to reveal to Jesuits what their vocation meant. According to Nadal, Ignatius' story was their story, the story of the ideal Jesuit whose virtues and life-choices they were called to emulate. In telling the story, Nadal took it beyond the *Acta* to narrate the founding of the order so as to present Ignatius as *the* founder, minimizing the role Ignatius' companions played in the years before the official papal approbation of the Society.

In presenting Ignatius to his fellow Jesuits, Nadal therefore implicitly equated Ignatius with saintly founders like Dominic and Francis. He at the same time made Ignatius into a Counter-Reformation figure by portraying him as the David raised up by divine providence to slay Luther, the new Goliath, enemy of God's people. In 1555, the year before Ignatius died, Nadal had made his first trip to Germany, where he was shocked by the desperate situation of the church, and he began vigorously to propagate the view that the Society had a providential responsibility for remedying the situation.[26] Although Ignatius never felt the slightest sympathy for the Reformation, he gave it only peripheral attention until toward the end of his life, and he scarcely mentioned it in the *Acta*.[27] Through Nadal, however, the myth that the Jesuits were founded to oppose the Reformation entered the historiographical tradition, where it sank roots so deep that scholarship seems powerless to eradicate it.

Ribadeneyra's Biography

From Nadal, most Jesuits became familiar with the basic story, at least in outline form. Many of them wanted a more complete account, something they could hold in their hands and read. As early as 1546, while Ignatius was still alive and vigorous, Ribadeneyra had already proposed the idea of a biography to Diego de Eguía, Ignatius' confessor. Eguía put him off by saying there was no need because the four evangelists had already written it.[28] Ignatius, a Christ-figure!

The issue did not go away. In 1558, two years after Ignatius's death, a talented young Spanish Jesuit, Pedro Juan Perpinyá, wanted to write a biography of Ignatius, a project Nadal encouraged, but Perpinyá died before being able to pursue it. Meanwhile requests came to Laínez, who in 1558 succeeded Ignatius as superior general, for a "well written life of our father Ignatius." Laínez replied in one instance that "action will be taken at the appropriate time," but, perhaps because he was relying on Perpinyá's initiative, he in fact did nothing.

In 1565 Francisco de Borja succeeded Laínez as general, and the following year Perpinyá died. The next year, 1567, Borja commissioned Ribadeneyra to write a proper biography.[29] He then asked all the houses and provinces of the Society to send him whatever materials they possessed that related to the project, including copies of the *Acta*. He put this material at Ribadeneyra's disposal. In calling in these materials, he removed the *Acta* (and correlative documents like Laínez' letter of 1547) from circulation, which meant "the pilgrim's story" lay almost unknown until printed for the first time in the early twentieth century.

Borja seems to have envisaged a biography that would be definitive, making other accounts, even the *Acta*, superfluous, and ensuring that misinformation not circulate. Borja, Ribadeneyra, and other leading Jesuits were intent on presenting to members of the Society and eventually to the world at large a literary portrait of Ignatius that would be as free of factual error as humanly possible. This does not mean, of course, that they wanted a dispassionate account, for they clearly wanted one that portrayed Ignatius and with him the Society as positively as possible Such an account would, besides showing forth Ignatius as the saintly person they held him to be, vindicate against the Society's enemies its legitimacy in the church.

Ribadeneyra was an obvious choice, and not simply because he had years earlier raised the issue. He was an excellent stylist in both Latin and Spanish, which professionally qualified him for the task because until the nineteenth century, the discipline that trained historians was rhetoric. Borja's decision was vindicated by Ribadeneyra's subsequent career as a writer. By the end of his life, Ribadeneyra had produced a long list of publications, mostly of a historical and biographical nature, that were successes, indeed, sometimes extraordinary successes in the marketplace.

He had, moreover, been on especially close terms with Ignatius since his youth. Born in 1526 into a wealthy and well-placed "New Christian" family of Toledo, he was commended in the spring of 1539 by his mother to Cardinal Alessandro Farnese, the grandson of the then reigning Pope Paul III, who was in Spain for the obsequies of the Empress Isabella, wife of Charles V. The cardinal brought the boy to Rome as a page in his household. Much later in life, Ribadeneyra described himself at that stage as "restless, naughty and impetuous, free-spirited and spoiled."[30] For reasons he never fully explained but that probably had to do with some prank or altercations with other young members of the cardinal's retinue, he ran away and through Doctor Pedro Ortiz, a friend of the Jesuits, ended up in the Jesuit residence. In September, 1540, Ignatius received him into the Society, ten days before Paul III officially approved the order. Ribadeneyra was thirteen years old.

He died only in 1611, after an astounding seventy-one years in the Society of Jesus during which he at only one point wavered in the commitment he made when he had barely entered his teens. The depth of the commitment was surely due in large part to the extraordinarily close bond he formed with Ignatius from the first moment. He revered Ignatius, knew him well, and felt deep affection for him. Ignatius responded in kind, almost as if Ribadeneyra were the son he never had. Many decades later, Ribadeneyra in a moving prayer thanked God, who "gave me as a father and guide the blessed Ignatius . . . and . . . infused him with such an extraordinary and concerned love for me . . . and . . . from the very first time I met and talked to him, gave me a recip-rocal love for him."[31] After Ribadeneyra had spent two years in the same house with Ignatius and other Jesuits in Rome, Ignatius sent him to Paris to study, and, when the political situation there grew too hot for Spaniards, he sent him to Louvain and then in 1545 to the University of Padua.

Just a few years later, Ribadeneyra began holding important offices in the Society, especially in the Low Countries and Italy, where he was successively provincial of Tuscany and then of Sicily. In 1574 he returned to Spain for the first time since his childhood. He remained there for the rest of his life. His return was ostensibly for reasons of health, but it fitted into the anti-Spanish sentiments of the General Congregation of 1573 that elected the first non-Spanish superior general, the Belgian Everard Mercurian, and that resulted in departures of Spaniards from the Jesuit curia and from Italy more broadly.

A few years earlier, in 1569, while Borja was still general, Ribadeneyra brought his finished Latin manuscript to Rome. As he stated in the prologue, while writing the book he decided to make a conspectus of the history of the order until the death of Ignatius part of it. The manuscript was subjected to a searching examination by a number of Jesuits who also knew Ignatius personally, including Peter Canisius and Ignatius' cousin, Antonio de Araoz.[32] It is not clear how many changes Ribadeneyra made in his text as a result of these consultations or *censurae*, as they were called. Canisius, for instance, wanted greater scope given to the role played by some of the original companions of Paris, yet he was enthusiastic about what Ribadeneyra had accomplished: "The work cannot be praised too highly."[33]

Ribadeneyra's admiration for Ignatius was unbounded and uncritical. The care he and his "censors" took to render the *Vita* as factually accurate as possible is important, but the book is hagiography, pure and simple, and it reinforced an earlier tendency to interpret every aspect of Ignatius' life in the most glowing terms. Nicholas Bobadilla, who, though one of the original companions, had an intermittently difficult relationship with Ignatius, complained to Pope Paul IV in 1557 that Laínez, Nadal, and Polanco "want to treat everything Father Master Ignatius did or said as if it were a revelation of the Holy Spirit."[34] Bobadilla was, however, a lonely voice.

In a print-run of 500 copies, Ribadeneyra's *Vita Ignatii Loiolae, Societatis Iesu Fundatoris* was published in Naples in 1572. Circulation was restricted to Jesuits, again, it seems, to allow Jesuits to examine it before making it available to the world at large. Borja himself, however, did not strictly observe the restriction but gave copies as gifts to a few friends of the Society. Among the Jesuits satisfaction with the book seems to have been general.

The care with which it was reviewed should have ensured its acceptance as standard. When Borja died later that year, the book was read at table during the General Congregation that elected his successor. What greater success could Ribadeneyra have hoped for! Yet a year later the newly elected Mercurian prohibited its further publication and distribution, and he commissioned an Italian Jesuit, Giampietro Maffei, to write another biography of Ignatius. As Borja had done earlier, Mercurian put all the relative materials at Maffei's disposal. Maffei had qualifications for his commission in that he had taught rhetoric and had translated into Latin from Portuguese the first history of Jesuit missions in Asia, written by Manuel da Costa. But he entered the Society only in 1565, nine years after Ignatius' death.[35]

What was going on? Although the general anti-Spanish sentiment in many parts of the Society probably had something to do with it, it can hardly have been the principal motive at work. The decision is best explained by putting it into the context of the maneuvers of some Spanish Jesuits to achieve more independence from Roman central government. The maneuvers or machinations, potentially schismatic, were an attack on the high degree of authority wielded by the general. Rumors spread that Ribadeneyra was deeply involved in the agitation, and Mercurian seems to have believed them.[36] Only after some years did Mercurian become persuaded of Ribadeneyra's innocence.

Maffei, who had his own troubles with Mercurian, had completed his biography in 1579, but in a trip through Spain he discovered new material and asked Mercurian to defer publication. When Mercurian died the next year,

Maffei's book was therefore still unpublished. Meanwhile, Ribadeneyra had revised his book, amplified it somewhat, and translated it into Spanish. He again sent it to Rome for the new general to review. By this time Claudio Aquaviva, a young, talented, energetic Neapolitan nobleman, had succeeded Mercurian. Aquaviva gave Ribadeneyra's Spanish text strong support, which led to its publication in 1583.

When Maffei finally published his version of Ignatius' life in 1585, Aquaviva wrote an introductory letter for it, showing that he was ready to tolerate multiple interpretations, though it is clear he preferred Ribadeneyra's. Maffei's work, in Latin, was published almost simultaneously in Rome, Venice, and Cologne and went through a number of subsequent printings into the middle of the eighteenth century, but was never translated into a vernacular.[37]

It was Ribadeneyra's biography that became canonical, due in large part to the popular demand for it. The book was almost instantaneously an international best-seller. During Ribadeneyra's lifetime, the Spanish text was republished six more times beginning in 1584, the year after it first appeared. Ribadeneyra's own Latin translation of it was published in 1586 in Madrid, republished in Antwerp in 1587, in Rome in 1589, in Ingolstadt in 1590, in Lyons in 1595, in Cologne in 1602. In 1586 an Italian translation from the Spanish was published in Venice, which was reprinted the following year. A German translation appeared at Ingolstadt in 1590, a French at Lyons in 1599, and an English by Michael Walpole at St. Omer's in 1616. The book was frequently republished in all these languages.

Without directly advertising itself as a "saint's life," that is precisely what it was. By the time it was published, the genre had been in crisis in certain parts of Europe for over a half-century. Erasmus and others mocked veneration of relics and saints as it had been traditionally practiced. When in 1523, for instance, Pope Adrian VI canonized Benno, an eleventh-century bishop of Meissen in Saxony, the event was celebrated there with a procession in which horse's bones were mockingly venerated as relics.[38] Luther wrote a pamphlet "Against the New Idol and the Old Devil About to Be Set up at Meissen." In time Protestants' disdain for holy people made exception especially for their own martyrs, with the result that Protestant traditions of hagiography, different yet also similar to Catholic, soon sprang up.[39]

Widespread among the cultural elites in the sixteenth century, no matter where they fell on the confessional scale, was a new concern for verifying assertions through examination of original documents. This concern was a species within the genus of the Renaissance humanists' cry for a "return to the sources," *ad fontes*. In fifteenth-century Italy writers like Flavio Biondo and Leonardo Bruni seized upon historians from classical antiquity as their models.

A more elegant Latin style was the most obvious way such writers differed from their medieval counterparts, but this shift in style was accompanied by shifts in purpose and even method. More attention was paid, for instance, to human motivation and less to supernatural causes.

For the humanists a history, whether secular or sacred, was moral philosophy teaching by example. According to them, it was full of ethical and political lessons applicable to contemporary circumstances. In that regard, therefore, the new historiography was consonant with traditional hagiography, which held up the saints as examples for imitation, as role-models. Alison Frazier has conclusively shown that the humanists of fifteenth-century Italy produced hundreds of lives of saints and that this production marked not so much a break with the medieval tradition as an intensified and, in some instances, a more self-critical continuation of it. The phenomenon was so wide-ranging in literary forms, authorial intent, and approach to sources to defy generalization, except that proper style was now a paramount concern. The rhetorician was the historian, and the result was "a literary Renaissance" for the saints.[40] David Collins has documented a similar Renaissance in Germany for roughly the same period.[41]

Erasmus' life of Jerome is the best known of those produced by humanists in the sixteenth century.[42] This *vita* was not meant to be a free-standing piece but to serve as the introduction to Erasmus' monumental edition of Jerome's works. Erasmus intended it as an entry-way into appreciation of Jerome's achievement as a scholar. As detached from that context, the life has been hailed as a break-through in hagiography because of the critical way Erasmus used his sources, his almost infallible instinct for dissociating fact from fiction, and his sober presentation. In Erasmus' life of Jerome, there were no miracles. The integrity of Jerome's life was proof enough of his sanctity.

Contained in the first volume of Erasmus' edition of Jerome's works, the *vita* was published in 1516, on the eve of the Reformation. It, along with Erasmus' well known satirical writings about the veneration of saints such as his colloquy "A Pilgrimage for Religion's Sake," acted as a prod and prelude to the reactions against the saints that broke out with the Reformation, and it helped create new perils facing authors who worked in the hagiographical genre. Although critical examination of sources by hagiographers did not begin in the Renaissance, it rose to a higher level and deviations from it were less well tolerated—at least for a while and in certain circles. These developments had even institutional impact, as suggested by the fact that for a period of sixty-five years, from 1523 until 1588, the popes canonized not a single saint.

In a hastily composed decree, the Council of Trent affirmed in one of its very last acts, 1563, the legitimacy, praiseworthiness, and spiritual advantages of veneration of the saints.[43] During that same Twenty-Fifth Session, it called for a revision of sacred texts, including the breviary, to correct errors and make sure of their orthodoxy.[44] For saints' feasts, the breviary contained in the "lessons" of the second nocturn of matins short biographies of the saint of the day, many of which did not measure up to the critical standards that were emerging. When Pope Sixtus V reorganized the Roman Curia in 1587-88, he created the Congregation of Sacred Rites and Ceremonies. Although the revision of the Roman Missal and breviary had been under way since the council concluded and work on the former completed under Pius V, the new Congregation continued to revise the breviary, including the second nocturns.

The Oratorian priest, Antonio Gallonio, a colleague of the much better known Cesare Baronio, left behind copious manuscripts that indicate the role he played in writing and revising lessons and prayers for the breviary for the Congregation, even though he was not an official member of it.[45] Evident in his notes is a concern for establishing an accurate chronology and for seeking out the oldest available manuscript sources for verifications. Like Ribadeneyra with his *Vida* of Ignatius, Gallonio is best known for writing the first life of Philip Neri, who would be canonized the same day as Ignatius.[46] He published the book only in 1601, long after Ribadeneyra's work, but in genre and concern for historical accuracy it was comparable to his.

Ribadeneyra divided his *Vida* of 1583 into five books. The first told Ignatius' story up to his arrival at the University of Paris in 1528, the second the story up to Pope Paul III's official approval of the new order in 1540. He construed the approval as a sign that "our Lord . . . had sent Father Ignatius into the world so that as a faithful minister he might serve the church and provide it with sons and soldiers to defend and protect it."[47] The third book begins with Ignatius' election as general in 1541 and takes the narrative up to about 1550, paying more attention to the general history of the order than to Ignatius himself, which is true for the most part also for book four, which ends with Ignatius' death.

In shifting the emphasis in books three and four to the order, Ribadeneyra set the pattern for future lives of Ignatius. The shift was almost inevitable. Once Ignatius became superior general, he virtually never stirred from Rome, and spent his days at his desk administering the order, which gave biographers little to work with. The years of action were over for Ignatius but just beginning for the Society.

The fifth book consisted of thirteen chapters, twelve of which deal with Ignatius' virtues. In the preface Ribadeneyra made clear that he was writing for Jesuits, and he presented Ignatius as perfectly fulfilling the high standards of virtue that the Ninth Part of the Jesuit *Constitutions* set for the general. The first chapter was about Ignatius' "gift of prayer and familiarity with God," the second about "his charity towards others," the third about "his humility," and so forth. The thirteenth was about his "miracles," which for Ribadeneyra are the testimony of his holy life and the great accomplishments God has worked through the Society. Those were miracle enough.[48]

Moving toward Canonization

Ribadeneyra's argument for Ignatius' sanctity is similar to Erasmus' for Jerome. But in fact Ribadeneyra was constrained to argue the way he did because at the time he wrote no miracles worked through Ignatius' intercession were known. The situation took on urgency just a few years after the *Vida* was first published. In 1588, Pope Sixtus V canonized Diego (Didacus) of Alcalá, thus ending the sixty-five-year hiatus. Canonizations were again possible. They were not, however, going to be a daily—or even an annual—occurrence. In the thirty-four years that elapsed between the canonization of Diego and the canonization of Ignatius in 1622, the popes bestowed the honor of universal cult, which is what canonization authorizes, on only five individuals. During the next thirty-seven years, 1622-58, only two saints would be canonized.[49]

In the very year Sixtus canonized Diego, moreover, he drastically reorganized the Roman Curia, which included, as mentioned, a new Congregation of Rites that had the supervision of canonization procedures. His action can be understood as a response to criticism, not only by Protestants, about the cult of the saints and about how individuals officially achieved the status of sainthood. Miracles, it was clear, would be required. The pressure was on. In 1591 Aquaviva wrote to Ribadeneyra that Ignatius' cause had not been able to go forward because the signs failed that God provided to ensure that his saints would be remembered. The "signs that failed" could only mean miracles.[50]

There were other problems. Clement VIII, who in 1592 succeeded Sixtus, was not particularly sympathetic toward the Society, and he happened to have a relatively long reign of thirteen years, until 1605. Besides, there was competition. In 1595, Philip Neri, the founder of the Oratorians, died. Though born in Florence, he spent most of his long life in Rome, where he was well-known to persons of every class of society, including the popes, and much beloved.

The Oratorians were as keen to have Philip canonized as the Jesuits were to have Ignatius.[51] If it came to a showdown between the two men, there was no doubt Philip would win. In Rome by the early seventeenth century, Ignatius was, except among the Jesuits, at best a distant memory and, besides, he was a Spaniard. Philip, on the contrary, was still vividly remembered and native-grown. Gallonio, Philip's biographer, was also the *procuratore* of the Oratorians for Philip, the person in the order responsible for promoting the cause

There was even competition within the Jesuit order itself. In 1552 Francis Xavier died off the coast of China after a short but spectacular career in India, Japan, and parts of present-day Indonesia. He was in the East at the behest of King John III of Portugal, who gave Xavier unstinting support during his whole missionary career. Xavier had electrified readers in Europe with his letters describing his activities. The first to be published was a long letter from India, January 15, 1544, of which both French and German translations appeared the next year.[52] Xavier was therefore much better known to a much wider public than Ignatius.

When King John heard of Xavier's death, he immediately ordered his viceroy in India to gather testimony in view of a future canonization. Between 1556-57 thirty-six eye-witness testimonies were taken in Goa alone. Xavier's corpse, exhumed months after his burial, was found perfectly fresh and incorrupt, though he had been buried with a large quantity of lime. Here was a striking and traditional indication of sanctity.[53]

For most Jesuits, proud as they were of Xavier, it would be unbecoming for him to be canonized before the founder. In their minds, however, the two men were closely linked, as is clear from a decree of the Jesuits' Fifth General Congregation, held in the winter of 1593-94, mandating Aquaviva, the general, to petition for the canonization of them both. The Sixth General Congregation, 1608, passed a similar decree.[54] Two years later Orazio Torsellino published in Rome a life of Xavier and a collection of his letters.[55] The volume was published that same year in Antwerp and within a short time translated into all the major European languages (English in 1632), as well as into Flemish and Hungarian. As it turned out, Xavier, though canonized the same day as Ignatius in 1622, was not declared a blessed until ten years after Ignatius, in 1619.

At the beginning of the century, the prospects for Ignatius' canonization had taken a turn for the better. In 1605, the new pope, Paul V, allowed the title of blessed to two youthful members of the Society, Aloysius Gonzaga and Stanislaus Kostka, which occurred just as the concept of beatification as distinct from canonization was more clearly emerging. This was an encouraging sign, though some Jesuits might have feared it as threatening to preempt Ignatius' canonization. Relations between the Oratorian cardinal, Cesare Baronio, and the Jesuit cardinal, Roberto Bellarmino, were cordial, which helped diffuse the Philip-Ignatius rivalry.

On the first anniversary of Philip's death, 1596, the Oratorians held a celebration at his tomb. The following year they held an even more elaborate one, in which the important cardinal of Milan, Federico Borromeo, who was in Rome on business, participated. This was a dangerous game for the Oratorians to play, because they could be accused of promoting public cult before having ecclesiastical approval. After a particularly splendid celebration in 1602, Pope Clement, still reigning, was furious, and the Oratorians knew they had overstepped the mark.

Nonetheless, their example seems to have encouraged the Jesuits to similar, though more cautious, actions. A paradox was at work here. While promoting public cult was forbidden, spontaneous cult was considered a sign of sanctity. Until 1599 Aquaviva had not allowed any ornamentation on Ignatius' tomb. That year, however, on the morning of July 31, the anniversary of Ignatius' death, Cardinal Bellarmino along with Cardinal Baronio appeared at the recently completed church of the Gesù. They both knelt in prayer before the tomb. Baronio kissed the floor in front of it and then climbed a ladder to affix a portrait of Ignatius above it. Then Bellarmino preached a sermon in praise of Ignatius. Their visit made a strong impression, of course, on people present in the church, who implicitly were invited to follow suite. The next day, the Duchess of Sessa, wife of the Spanish ambassador, sent three man-sized lamps to be installed at the tomb.

From that point on, a certain momentum began to build. On February 12 the next year, for instance, Baronio delivered a sermon that attracted a lot of attention in which he praised the Society of Jesus. Later that year, on July 31, he repeated in the Gesù what he had done the year before. That an Oratorian like Baronio would so publically promote the cause of the founder of the Jesuits called favorable attention to Ignatius in a way that no Jesuit could. Moreover, Baronio was a member of the Congregation of Rites, which meant that he was a voice for the cause from within the system.[56]

Engraving 77 in our *Vita* depicts a meeting between the two holy men, Philip and Ignatius. The caption says Philip often saw Ignatius' face resplendent with light, an indication of his sanctity. The relationship between the saints, who were probably little more than casual acquaintances, got expanded into a much closer relationship through pious legends. Nonetheless, that Philip said something about Ignatius close to what the caption indicates is well-founded. The Jesuits would, moreover, have been foolish to put the story forward so soon after Philip's death, when so many were alive who knew him, if it were not plausible.[57] This depiction of the two men in our *Vita* is meant to honor both, and it further suggests that the Oratorians and the Jesuits were now making common cause.

At this point Ribadeneyra once again came to Ignatius' rescue. In 1599 he published the first volume of a two-volume work of the lives of the saints, *Flos sanctorum.* Despite the title, the work was written in Spanish. At the end of the second volume, published two years later, he attached a much shorter, but still substantial version of his life of Ignatius. The implication was clear: Ignatius deserved to be in the same company as officially recognized saints. But this shorter biography was especially important because Ribadeneyra inserted into it the miracles that had previously been lacking and for which he now had the sworn testimonies collected for the process of his canonization. He was frank: "And because [without miracles] no saint is canonized and proposed by the Apostolic See to the whole church to be invoked and venerated, . . . I must here relate [for Ignatius] some miracles and extraordinary happenings such as we observe in the lives of other saints."[58]

In an edition of his *Vida* published after the *Flos sanctorum,* he at the end refers the reader to it. After again justifying his apologia for Ignatius' saintliness based on his holy life and the achievements of the Society he founded, Ribadeneyra added that after he wrote the *Vida* it pleased the Lord to make Ignatius' greatness known through "great and splendid" miracles (in the conventional sense). He felt obliged therefore to recount them in the biography he wrote for the *Flos.*[59]

In that new biography, he followed the same pattern as before—first a narration of Ignatius' life from Pamplona until his death, then a presentation of his great virtues, and finally the miracles, but now the miracles get expansive treatment. He adhered even here, however, to his principle of basing his account on solid evidence. For several decades sworn testimonies about Ignatius had been gathered as part of the process looking to his canonization, and many of these testimonies were about miracles performed through his intercession. It was from these documents—"*informaciones autenticas*"—that Ribadeneyra drew to make his case.[60]

In a short passage in the *Flos,* he extended a helping hand to the Oratorians by describing Philip Neri as "holy" and a man of "known sanctity" who founded the Oratory "of those venerable priests who have done so much good in Rome." Ribadeneyra, however, went way beyond the facts in saying that Philip was a "most devout child" of Ignatius and came to him for help "in all his doubts and troubles."[61]

The *Flos sanctorum* was organized according to saints' feast days in a calendar that began with January 1. After Ignatius was canonized, his entry was moved from being an add-on at the end of the second volume to July 31, his feast day. The book, which in a modern edition would run to well over 1,000 pages, was a spectacular publishing success, outstripping the *Vida.*[62] It appeared again in Madrid in 1604, in 1610, and in 1616, and it continued to be republished in Spanish into the eighteenth century. It hit the international market with translations into other vernaculars, including a translation into English as early as 1616, many times reprinted. It was almost immediately translated into French, and in that language had perhaps its biggest success. A Latin translation was published in 1630 and even earlier, a Japanese. Excerpted and augmented with contributions by other hagiographers, it was truly a best-seller published over and over again, with a renewed efflorescence in the nineteenth century.[63]

VISUAL REPRESENTATIONS OF IGNATIUS BEFORE THE *VITA*

The authors of our *Vita beati Ignatii Loiolae* were not the first to put Ignatius' story into visual form. If the Jesuits were from the beginning keen on committing the story to writing, they were just as keen in exploiting it for other media. Shortly after Ignatius' died, for instance, they had a death mask made and commissioned a portrait of him by the prominent Italian artist, Jacopo del Conte. These actions were just the beginning of the quest for a "true portrait" of the founder.[64]

Under the supervision of Ribadeneyra himself around the year 1600, Juan de Mesa painted a cycle of large oils for the Jesuit novitiate in Madrid. The paintings were not in this form available to a wide public, but later fourteen of the scenes were with a few changes in detail engraved in copper in Antwerp by Cornelis, Jan, and Theodore van Galle, Jan Collaert, and Karel van Mallery. The engravings appeared in 1610, the year after our *Vita*, and had wide circulation.[65] Probably slightly earlier the life had appeared with the twelve scenes engraved by Hieronymus Wierix, mentioned above.

An even earlier, much smaller, but still important depiction of Ignatius' story appeared in a copper engraving by famous portraitist Thomas de Leu, printed for the Jesuits in Paris in 1590.[66] In the center is a profile of Ignatius praying before a crucifix. He is surrounded by fifteen framed events from his life, with captions, most of which deal with his role as founder and superior of the order and thus include his gathering of the companions in Paris, his sending Xavier to India, and the approval of the order by Paul III. They also include, however, his healing at Loyola by Saint Peter, visions of Christ and Mary, his vision of Hoces, an early companion, in heaven. There are no miracles. The caption under his portrait reads: "Ignatius of Loyola. In the year of our Lord's Incarnation, 1540, he by a singular disposition of providence founded the religious order of the Society of Jesus at the time when Luther raged against the church. For the greater glory of God."

Far bolder was the copper engraving by another distinguished artist, Francesco Villamena. Rome, 1600. Ignatius kneels in an oval frame in the center, while behind his head irradiates a heavenly light, and similar streams of light descend upon him from a cloud and strike his breast. The caption underneath the portrait reads, "Blessed Ignatius, Founder of the Society of Jesus." In small oval frames surrounding the larger one are twenty-nine scenes, including miracles worked by Ignatius during his life and after his death. Each has a caption describing the action.

Villamena presents Ignatius as a recipient of visions from on high and as a miracle worker The scenes, detached from time and place, follow no logical or chronological order. They hardly relate Ignatius to the Society of Jesus, and, if the caption under his portrait were removed, he could be almost any visionary and thaumaturge at any time. The person depicted in the scenes had, however, an essential requirement for having his sanctity recognized, miracles.

It is astounding that such a work intended for a wide public and so blatantly portraying Ignatius as a saint would be produced during the reign of Clement VIII, a pope notably sensitive about organized promotion of a cult before ecclesiastical approval had been granted and not particularly well disposed toward the Jesuits. The dating, however, is certain, which means it appeared a year before Ribadeneyra's account of Ignatius' miracles in the second volume of the *Flos sanctorum*. Unfortunately, nothing is known about who sponsored the work or about the circumstances that gave rise to it except that Villamena dedicated it to Wilhelm V, Duke of Bavaria.[67] Wilhelm, who had abdicated in 1598, was the great patron of the Jesuits who built for them in Munich their magnificent Michaelskirche.[68]

Clement VIII did indeed react but relatively mildly. Aquaviva, in a letter of June 6, 1601, to Bernardo Confalonieri, provincial of the Roman province, said that the pope had ordered that no more copies of images of Ignatius with miracles be printed without his permission. Clement allowed those already printed, however, to continue to be sold in Rome. It fell to Confalonieri to see to it that the pope's order was carried out.[69]

VITA BEATI PATRIS IGNATII LOIOLAE

By 1605, therefore, Lancicius and Rinaldi did not lack resources for constructing their *Vita*. They had at their disposal the biographies by Ribadeneyra and Maffei, the *Flos sanctorum*, and the engraving by Villamena. They had access to Orlandini's manuscript on the history of the Society during Ignatius' lifetime and to the source upon which it was principally dependent, the massive "*Chronicon*" of those same years compiled by Juan Alfonso de Polanco, Ignatius' secretary.[70] Orlandini's and Polanco's works, more concerned with the larger Jesuit story than with Ignatius, would have provided the editors with little information about him not available to them in the published books.

Whether Lancicius and Rinaldi had access to other early, unpublished accounts, such as Ignatius' *Acta* or, if they did, whether they bothered to consult them, we do not know. Although it is impossible to sort out what they took directly from which source, the fact is that all but a handful of the seventy-nine scenes are found in some form in either Ribadeneyra's *Vida* or his *Flos sanctorum*. The editors needed to look no further, nor for the most part do we.

The foremost problem Lancicius and Rinaldi faced amid their embarrassment of riches was to decide the kind of story they would tell. That decision would determine their choice of events for the engravings. They had three basic options. The first was simply to tell the story of a holy man, a man whose life was resplendent with virtues and filled with special visitations from on high—basically the line taken by Ribadeneyra and Maffei in their biographies, which was consonant with the *Acta*. The second was Ignatius as miracle-worker, and here the *Flos* and the Villamena engraving would come to their aid. The third would be the story of the founder of the order, which would emphasize the events beginning with the gathering of the companions in Paris in the 1530s and provide images of such things as the approval of the order by Paul III and the sending of Xavier to India.

What they came up with was a combination of all three, but with the first predominating and providing the chronological framework for the other two. The first fifty-five images illustrate for the most part events Ignatius himself relates in his *Acta*, the story of conversion and spiritual growth. The very first image, however, deviates from the *Acta*, from the other early unpublished sources, from the biographies by Ribadeneyra and Maffei, and from the *Flos*. It depicts Ignatius' birth in a stable outside the castle of Loyola. His mother, the caption tells us, had ordered the servants to take her there. The image is meant to convey the deep piety of the family into which Ignatius was born, a standard *topos* in hagiography, but it does much more by likening the situation of Ignatius' birth to that of Jesus himself.

Some of the authentic stories are embellished or sanitized. Ignatius in the *Acta* frankly tells how as a student he was imprisoned in Alcalá and Salamanca under suspicion of heresy and in the former city interrogated by the Inquisition. The caption for image 30, which depicts Ignatius behind bars, states simply that in both places he "suffered calumnies for the sake of Christ" and was put in jail. That was the truth but not the whole truth. Image 61, however, accurately depicts, almost precisely as he describes it in the *Acta*, how a decade later in Rome he was absolved of charges.

Another incident developed into a miracle. Laínez' letter of 1547, Polanco's "commentary," Ignatius's *Acta*, Ribadeneyra's *Vida*, and our *Vita* all recount how Simâo Rodrigues, one of the companions from Paris, recovered from a life-threatening illness in 1537 when Ignatius, though sick himself, made, with Pierre Favre, another of the original companions, the day-long journey on foot from Vicenza to Bassano to visit him. Laínez in his letter of 1547 says that during the journey Ignatius became aware Simon would return to health, and when he arrived at Bassano he predicted to Simon that he was not going to die.[71] In his "summary" the following year, Polanco does not mention the prediction, but says that from the moment Ignatius and Favre arrived at where Simon was staying, Simon began to improve, which meant God heard the prayers his servants had poured out to him.[72] A few years later when Ignatius dictated the Acta, he said that along the way to Bassano God gave him the assurance that Simon would not die, which he revealed to his companion Favre, and that when the two arrived on the scene Simon was consoled and quickly recovered.[73]

In the *Vida,* Ribadeneyra justifies his account of the incident by saying that he heard about it from Laínez, to whom Favre told the story shortly after it happened, yet Ribadeneyra's account goes beyond what Laínez reported in 1547. Ribadeneyra says that Ignatius reassured Favre about Rodrigues and that when the two of them arrived at the scene they found Simon still gravely ill. Ignatius then embraced him, told him not to fear, and assured him he would recover. "And thus he got up and was well" (*y assí se levantó y estuvo bueno*).[74] In the concluding chapter of the book, however, he says straightforwardly that "he healed Father Simon from his dangerous illness" (*aver sanado al padre Simón de su peligrosa enfermedad*).[75]

Image 50 of the *Vita* carries the healing a small step further. On a table in the sickroom stand a cross, lighted candle, and a small cruet presumably holding sacred oil, indicating that Simon, who lies with eyes closed on the bed, has received the last rites. Ignatius is shown embracing him. Favre stands behind Ignatius with hands folded in prayer. Through a window off to the left, Ignatius is seen on his knees with a ray of light descending toward him, the divine inspiration that assured him of Simon's recovery. The caption reads: "His companion Simâo Rodrigues was close to death, but, though he himself was suffering from a fever, he quickly hastens to make a journey of eighteen Roman miles and heals him with an embrace." The miracle is not a story introduced from non-canonical sources but the result of a gradual refashioning of authentic accounts.

It would be tedious to review here the engravings to show how faithful or unfaithful they are to the sources, but the above examples give an indication of how slippage occurred between the verbal and the visual and even between different verbal versions of the same event. As mentioned in the preface to this facsimile edition, for each of the scene I have indicated the relevant passages, if they exist, from two major sources—the *Acta*, and the *Vida*. From the *Flos sanctorum*, I indicate passages, generally miracles, only when they are not found in the other two. For anyone who wants to examine a particular image against the written tradition, the passages I have indicated provide the essential first step.

In such a scrutiny, allowance must of course be made for the simplification that a brief caption and the visual medium require. Figure 39 depicts Ignatius gathering the nine companions at Paris who would be the nucleus of the new Society of Jesus, and figure 41 depicts the ten of them in 1534 pronouncing their vow to go to Jerusalem together, which was the crucial step that in 1539 led to their decision to stay together and found a new religious order. In fact, as Ribadeneyra makes clear in the *Vida*, Ignatius gathered only six companions and with him only six pronounced the vow in 1534. The other three—Claude Jay, Paschase Broët, and Jean Codure–joined the group only after Ignatius left Paris, but then all ten were reunited in Italy in 1537 to become founders. This is a story that can be told through pictures only by simplifying it.

A different kind of adjustment occurs in figure #17. In the *Acta,* Ignatius tells how at mass in the Dominican church in Manresa he saw "with his inward eye" rays of light coming from the sacred host at the moment of elevation, and how he saw "with his understanding" (*entendimiento*) how Christ was present in the sacrament.[76] In his *Vida*, Ribadeneyra accurately reports the event (*con los ojos del alma*).[77] What Ignatius experienced was an internal illumination, an insight, not a vision. But how portray in visual form an intellectual experience? The artist for image #17 had little choice but to turn it into a vision. The caption then takes the depiction literally, ". . . in the sacred host he saw Christ the Lord with his eyes." (A large oil painting, attributed to Andrea Commodi, probably sometime between 1605 and 1608, produced for the Farnese Chapel in the Gesù, did the same.[78])

Nonetheless, despite the occasional retouching, the events depicted in the *Vita*, if we except the miracles, are fundamentally faithful to the earliest sources and to the portrait drawn by Ribadeneyra in the *Vida* of 1583. Fundamentally faithful, yes, but would the retouching have been tolerated earlier? Beginning in 1547 with Polanco's request to Laínez for an account of the origins of the Society, the Jesuits showed an almost obsessive concern for accuracy of detail about Ignatius' life, a concern that prompted the meticulous review in 1572 by his fellow Jesuits of Ribadeneyra's Latin text. Would they have tolerated the first image, Ignatius' birth in a stable, which is a later fabrication?

The Jesuits, in any case, never shared the skepticism of Erasmus, the Protestant Reformers, and others about miracles, visions, and transports. The *Vita* is replete with supernal interventions of various kinds. At least fourteen of the images portray Ignatius seeing visions—of Christ, the saints, or the devil. He is the object of the special protection of Providence. He has a gift of prophesy and of levitation; he receives special internal illuminations from on high; and he successfully performs exorcisms. All these are happenings beyond normal human experience, but they are not miracles as such. Many of them have at least a foundation in the *Acta.*

Only seven images clearly portray Ignatius as a wonder-worker, that is, as himself effecting some occurrence for the better that transcends what are sometimes called the laws of nature. In one of them he appears in a vision to a Jesuit in Cologne (#76). In the remaining six he restores somebody to health (#45, 47, 48, 50, 74), or somebody is restored to health through a relic, in this instance through a piece of his clothing taken from his body before burial (#78).

If seven depict him as miracle-worker, a slightly larger number directly show Ignatius as the founder of the Society. Small though that number is, they succeed in integrating the story of him as founder into the story of the holy man and the wonder-worker. He gathers, as mentioned, the nine companions in Paris (#39), and they pronounce the vow to go to Jerusalem (#41). In 1540, Paul III approves their proposal for the new order (#56). Ignatius sends Xavier to "the Indies" (#57). After Ignatius was elected superior in 1541, the companions pronounce their vows as Jesuits (58). Xavier with affection and reverence writes to Ignatius from the Indies (#59). At the urging of Ignatius, Pope Julius III founds the German College (#64). Ignatius writes the Jesuit *Constitutions* (#65).

The first two of these events were important and uncontested facts, and the remaining six were matter of public record. If allowance is made for the simplification that brief captions and the visual medium required, these eight stand up well to scrutiny against the sources. The depiction of the founding of the German College is a good instance of the shorthand. Ignatius, not Pope Julius III, has to be reckoned as the real founder of the German College, though he did not go ahead with it until Pope Julius approved and promised financial assistance. On one level, it is curious that the founding of the German College is commemorated while its parent institution, the incomparably more important Roman College, gets no notice. But on another, it is understandable. Singling out the German College allowed the editors to insinuate the Jesuits' campaign against the Reformation while still focusing attention on Ignatius' life in Rome.

It is, however, the title page that most effectively presents Ignatius as founder, as a holy father of holy sons. The iconographic program is superimposed on a sturdy architectural structure decorated with a number of medallions or cartouches on which are portraits of Jesuits, all but four of whom—Ignatius, Xavier, Gonzaga, and Kostka—died violent deaths and hence were reckoned martyrs. In the middle of the structure hangs a curtain on which is inscribed the official monogram of the Society, IHS (Jesus). Under the monogram, the title reads, "The Life of Blessed Father Ignatius of Loyola, Founder of the Society of Jesus. Rome. 1609." At the top of the page, above the architecture, is a small semi-profile portrait of Ignatius, who is not explicitly identified except that he is the only figure with a halo. On either side of him two reclining putti hold a scroll with the words "Neither roses nor lilies are lacking among his flowers" (*Floribus eius nec rosae nec lilia desunt*). The words can be less literally and more pointedly translated as "In his garden both roses and lilies grow in abundance"—symbols of love and purity, respectively.

Immediately under Ignatius is a medallion with a semi-profile portrait of "Blessed Francis Xavier," by far the best known of all the Jesuits, for whose canonization, as mentioned, the momentum had begun as soon as news of his death reached Europe a half-century earlier. In the *Vida*, Ribadeneyra of course devotes a long passage to him.[79] On either side of Xavier are medallions with Aloysius Gonzaga and Stanislaus Kostka, whom Paul V had just beatified. Aloysius, as the eldest son of the Marquis Ferrante Gonzaga, a cousin of the duke of Mantua, was destined to bear the title Marchese Imperiale di Castiglione, which he renounced when in 1585 he entered the Jesuits. He died after only six years in the Society, before ordination, from the lingering effects of illness contracted while nursing plague victims. Stanislaus, from a noble and wealthy Polish family, died as a novice in Rome in 1568, at the age of eighteen, after being in the order less than a year. Although neither of them would be canonized until the eighteenth century, they were from this point forward ubiquitous staples of Jesuit iconographic self-presentation, invariably paired.

Then under Xavier appear three figures identified as "Blessed Rodolfo Aquaviva and companions." Aquaviva, missionary to India, was a son of the Duke of Atri and a nephew of Claudio Aquaviva, the superior general. He was in charge of the first Jesuit mission to the Mughal emperor Akbar. After three years at Akbar's court, he returned to Goa, the Portuguese capital in India. That same year, in the village of Cuncolim in the Salsette peninsula, he, four other Jesuits, and some Portuguese laymen, were attacked by a Portuguese-hating (and therefore Christian-hating) mob and killed. In the *Vida*, Ribadeneyra holds him up as among the holy martyrs who give proof of the miracle of the Society.[80]

At the center of the base of the structure are depicted two ships and several figures in the water, under which is inscribed, "Forty Martyrs." The allusion is to the most tragic loss of life the Jesuits suffered in the sixteenth century. In 1570, forty of them sailing to Brazil as missionaries under the leadership of the Portuguese nobleman, Ignacio de Azevedo, were intercepted by the Huguenot corsair, Jacques Sourie (Soria, Sore). When Sourie discovered who they were, he ordered them executed and their bodies cast into the sea. As soon as word of their fate reached Catholic Europe, they were celebrated as martyrs, as of course does Ribadeneyra in the *Vida*. (Though Azevedo was of noble blood, he was illegitimate, the son of a priest and a Benedictine nun.)[81]

To the left under the column is a medallion with three figures hanging on crosses with the inscription "in Japan." At Nagasaki on February 5, 1597, the war lord Toyotomi Hideyoshi ordered the execution of a Japanese Jesuit, "Paulo" Miki, and two Japanese lay helpers of the Jesuits. This brutal event, at which six Franciscans and their lay helpers were also executed, presaged the massive persecution a few decades later, the end of "the Christian century" in Japan, when between 1617 and 1622 thirty-four Jesuits were executed.

In the corresponding medallion on the right over the inscription "in Florida." stands a group of Jesuits holding martyrs' palms. In 1566, the Jesuits first arrived in Florida. That very year, Pedro Martínez, leader of a group of three, was killed by the Amerindians somewhere near St. Johns River in Florida.[82] The other two escaped. Four years later, a group of eight Jesuits in an ill-fated mission led by Juan Bautista de Segura returned to "Florida," sailed into the Chesapeake Bay, and disembarked near College Creek, Virginia. Within less than five months, on February 4 and 9, 1571, they too all died at the hands of the natives. Ribadeneyra of course celebrates them.[83]

Three pairs of medallions hang alongside the outer columns of the structure. In the first pair is a portrait on the left of Antonio Criminali, who was killed at Vedalai, India, in an attack on a Portuguese garrison by Badagas troops as he tried to aid the Christian women and children. The incident took place in June, 1549. The early date meant Criminali was looked upon as the first martyr, the "proto-martyr," of the Society, which is how Ribadeneyra in the *Vida* describes him.[84] On the opposite side is Edmund Campion, the English Jesuit, a convert from the Anglican church in which he had been ordained a deacon, who was executed under Elizabeth in London in 1581. Ribadeneyra mentions him along with Thomas Cottam, executed the following year.[85]

Beneath on the left is a profile of Abraham Francisco de Georgiis. Born in Syria into a Maronite family, he entered the Society after studying at the Roman College. A missionary, he was beheaded by the Muslim governor of Eritrea in 1595. On the right are the profiles of two French Jesuits, Jacques Salès and Guillaume Saultemouche, who in 1593 were arrested by Huguenots at Aubenas (Ardèche) and after exchanges with them principally about the Eucharist, were executed.[86]

The title page thus presents Ignatius as the progenitor of saints and martyrs. They were all figures from the half-century just passed, and a number of them had died within recent memory. The program for the title page could not have been grounded more solidly in the contemporary reality of Catholicism or suggest more vividly its universal mission and its vitality in the midst of tribulations. In it as nowhere else in this little volume, Ribadeneyra's consistent refrain that the founding of the Society of Jesus was Ignatius' real miracle found effective visual expression. The next page contains a bust-portrait of Ignatius in an oval frame under the IHS monogram. The inscription under the portrait, a conflation from Ecclesiasticus and Isaiah, gives verbal utterance to the visual message of the frontispiece: "In every work he gave witness to the Holy One, and from the ends of the earth he brought his brothers as a gift to the Lord."

NOTES

I am grateful to David Collins, Simon Ditchfield, and Walter Melion for their suggestions and criticisms on early drafts of this introduction.

FN = *Fontes narrativi de S. Ignatio de Loyola et de Societatis Iesu initiis*, ed. Cándido de Dalmases, 4 vols., Monumenta Historica Societatis Iesu 66, 73, 85, 93 (Rome: Monumenta Historica Societatis Iesu, 1943-65).

1. *Vita et miracula Sancti Francisci de Paula* (Rome: s.n., 1584).
2. *D. Catharinae Senesis virginis ss.mae ord. Praedicatorum vita ac miracula selectiora formis aeneis expressa* (Antwerp: Philips Galle, 1603).
3. *Vita s. Ioannis Baptistae graphice descripta* (Antwerp: Collaert, n.d.).
4. *Vita et miracula seraphici patris s. Francisci de Assisio* (Rome, 1608).
5. See Ursula König-Nordhoff, "Zur Entstehungsgeschichte der Vita beati P. Ignatii Loiolae Societatis Iesu Fundatoris Romae 1609 und 1622," *Archivum Historicum Societatis Iesu* 45 (1976), 306-17, at 312.
6. Niccolò Orlandini and Francesco Sacchini, *Historiae Societatis Iesu, prima pars sive Ignatius* (Rome: apud B. Zannettum, 1614).
7. See FN 3:639-721, as well as ibid., 420-39. See also the entry "Lęczycki" in Charles E. O'Neill and Joaquín M. Domínguez, eds., *Diccionario Histórico de la Compañía de Jesús*, 4 vols. (Rome: Institutum Historicum Societatis Iesu and Madrid: Universidad Pontificia Comillas, 2001), 3:2317. His unpublished writings about Ignatius are collected in FN 3:639-721. On his spiritual teaching, see Joseph de Guibert, *The Jesuits, Their Spiritual Doctrine and Practice: A Historical Study*, trans. William J. Young (Chicago: Institute of Jesuit Sources, 1964), 338-39. On the *Gloria S. Ignatii*, see FN 3:696-98.
8. See Ursula König-Nordhoff, *Ignatius von Loyola: Studien zur Entwicklung einer neuen Heiligen-Ikonographie im Rahmen einer Kanonisationskampagne um 1600* (Berlin: Gebr. Mann, 1982), 118-21, 277-324, especially 304-5. Lancicius in a short document "Memorabilia de S. Ignatio," 1634, says that he and Rinaldi were the editors of the book, FN 3:701-15, at 707. König-Nordhoff, "Entstehungsgeschichte," corrected errors in Julius S. Held, "Rubens and the Vita Beati P. Ignatii Loiolae of 1609," in *Rubens before 1620*, ed. John Rupert Martin (Princeton: Art Museum, Princeton University, 1972), 93-134.

9. König-Nordhoff, *Ignatius*, provides, passim, the fullest account of Barbé's career and oeuvre.

10. See ibid., 305 and n. 62.

11. See Jerome Nadal, *Annotations and Meditations on the Gospels*, trans. Frederick A. Homann, S.J., introductions by Walter Melion, 3 vols. (Philadelphia: Saint Joseph's University Press, 2003).

12. See ibid., 257-59.

13. See ibid., 301-5.

14. See ibid., 80-87.

15. See John Rupert Martin, *The Ceiling Paintings for the Jesuit Church in Antwerp*, 2 vols. (London and New York: Phaidon, 1968), and now Anna C. Knaap, "Meditation, Ministry, and Visual Rhetoric in Peter Paul Rubens's Program for the Jesuit Church in Antwerp," in *The Jesuits II: Cultures, Sciences, and the Arts, 1540-1773*, ed. John W. O'Malley, et al. (Toronto: University of Toronto Press, 2006), 157-81.

16. FN 1:54-145.

17. Ibid., 1:146-298.

18. See Cándido de Dalmases, "Prolegomena," FN 4:3-54 See also Françoise Durand, "La première historiographie ignatienne," in *Ignacio de Loyola y su tiempo: Congreso internacional de historia*, ed. Juan Plazaola (Bilbao: Universidad de Deusto, c. 1992), 23-36; Jos E. Vercruysse, "L'historiographie ignatienne aux XVI-XVIII siècles," ibid., 37-54; Rafael Olaechea, "Historiografía ignaciana del siglo XVIII," ibid., 55-105; John W. O'Malley, "The Historiography of the Society of Jesus: Where Does It Stand Today?" in *The Jesuits: Cultures, Sciences, and the Arts, 1540-1773*, ed. John W. O'Malley, et al. (Toronto: University of Toronto Press, 1999), 3-37; Franco Motta, "Alle origini della Compagnia di Gesù: La Compagine sacra, Elementi di un mito delle origini nella storiografia sulla Compagnia di Gesù," *Rivista Storica Italiana* 117 (2005), 5-25; and Motta, "Il serpente e il fiore del frassino: L'identità della Compagnia di Gesù come processo di autolegittimazione," in *Nunc alia tempora, alii mores: Storici e storia in età postridentina*, ed. Massimo Firpo (Firenze: Olschki, 2005), 189-210. Guido Mongoni's conspiratorial insinuations weaken rather than strengthen his argument "Censura e identità nella prima storiografia gesuitica (1547-1572)," also in Firpo, *Nunc alia tempora*, 169-88. For anti-Jesuit literature in the modern era, see, e.g., Geoffrey Cubitt, *The Jesuit Myth: Conspiracy Theory and Politics in Nineteenth-Century France* (Oxford: Clarendon Press, 1993), and Róisín Healy, *The Jesuit Specter in Imperial Germany* (Boston and Leiden: Brill Academic Publishers, 2003).

19. FN 2:506-97. For a list of Polanco's mistakes, see ibid., 508.

20. See ibid., e.g., 517, 519, 536.

21. See John W. O'Malley, *The First Jesuits* (Cambridge, MA: Harvard University Press, 1993), 287-96.

22. See Nadal's "*Praefatio*," at the bottom of the pages, FN 1:354-63.

23. On him see the "Introduction" to Luís Gonçaves da Câmara, *Remembering Iñigo: Glimpses of the Life of Saint Ignatius of Loyola, The Memoriale of Luís Gonçalves da Câmara*, trans. and ed. Alexander Eaglestone and Joseph A Munitiz (Saint Louis: Institute of Jesuit Sources, 2004).

24. Ribadeneyra, letter to Nadal, October 24, 1567, *Epistolae P. Hieronymi Nadal Societatis Iesu ab anno 1546 ad 1577*, 4 vols. (Madrid: Avrial, 1898-1905), 3:540.

25. FN 5:135, now in English as *A Brief and Exact Account: The Recollections of Simâo Rodrigues on the Origin and Progress of the Society of Jesus*, trans. Joseph F. Conwell (St. Louis: Institute of Jesuit Sources, 2004).

26. See O'Malley, *First Jesuits*, 272-83.

27. See ibid., 278-79.

28. See the *Memoriale Romanum,* FN 3:722-43, at 737: "...la vita de M. Ignatio està escripta ya per li quatro evangeliste et per la Sacra Scriptura, perchè non cè che una vita, sicut unus Christus, una fides, unum baptisma." See Ephesians 4:5.

29. On Perpinyá, Laínez, and Borja, see Cándido de Dalmases' "Prolegomena," FN 4:4-12. On Ribadeneyra, see O'Neill, *Diccionario,* 4:3345-3346; Jodi Bilinkoff, "The Many 'Lives' of Pedro de Ribadeneyra," *Renaissance Quarterly* 52 (1999), 180-96; and David J. Collins, "Life After Death: A Rhetorical Analysis of Pedro de Ribadeneyra's *Vida del padre Ignacio de Loyola, Fundador de la Compañía de Jesus,*" STL Thesis, Weston Jesuit School of Theology (Cambridge, MA, 1998).

30. As quoted in Bilinkoff, "Many 'Lives,'" 190.

31. As quoted ibid., 180.

32. For these "censures," see FN 4:933-98.

33. Ibid., 4:944-52, at 951.

34. *Epistolae Nadal,* 4:733, " . . . vogliano che tutte le cose del P. M. Ignatio siano come revellatione dello Spirito Sancto." See O'Malley, *First Jesuits,* pp. 308-9.

35. See O'Neill, *Diccionario,* 3:2466-2467.

36. See Francisco de Borja Medina, "Everard Mercurian and Spain: Some Burning Issues," in *The Mercurian Project: Forming Jesuit Culture, 1573-1580,* ed. Thomas M. McCoog (St. Louis: Institute of Jesuits Sources, and Rome: Institutum Historicum Societatis Iesu, 2004), 945-66, at 950.

37. For the strange story of the interaction of these two authors, see FN 3:208-36. See also König-Nordhoff, *Ignatius,* 48-53.

38. See Peter Burke, "How to be a Counter-Reformation Saint," in the collection of his articles, *The Historical Anthropology of Early Modern Italy: Essays on Perception and Communication* (Cambridge: Cambridge University Press, 1987), 48-62, at 49-50; and David J. Collins, *Reforming Saints: Saints' Lives and Their Authors in Germany 1470-1530* (New York: Oxford University Press, 2008), 3-6.

39. See, e.g., Brad S. Gregory, *Salvation at Stake: Christian Martyrdom in Early Modern Europe* (Cambridge, MA: Harvard University Press, 1999).

40. See Alison Knowles Frazier, *Possible Lives: Authors and Saints in Renaissance Italy* (New York: Columbia University Press, 2005), 317.

41. See Collins, *Reforming Saints.*

42. See David J. Collins, "A Life Reconstituted: Jacobus de Voragine, Erasmus of Rotterdam, and Their Lives of St. Jerome," *Medievalia et Humanistica: Studies in Medieval and Renaissance Culture,* NS 25 (1998), 31-51.

43. See Norman P. Tanner, ed., *Decrees of the Ecumenical Councils,* 2 vols. (Washington: Georgetown University Press, 1990), 2:774-76.

44. See ibid., 2:797.

45. See Simon Ditchfield, "'Historia Magistra Sanctitatis'? The Relationship between Historiography and Hagiography in Italy after the Council of Trent (1561-1742 ca.)," in *Firpo, Nunc alia tempora,* 3-23.

46. Antonio Gallonio, *Vita del beato padre Filippo Neri fiorentino* (Rome: Luigi Zannetti, 1601).

47. FN 4:310-11.

48. FN 4:900-31.

49. Simon Ditchfield generously allowed me to read and make use of his unpublished paper, "'Coping with the *beati moderni': Canonisation Procedure in the Aftermath of the Council of Trent."

50. See König-Nordhoff, *Ignatius*, 38. For detailed discussion of the measures taken by the Jesuits to promote Ignatius and of the problems they encountered, see ibid., 33-42.

51. See A. D. Wright, "'A Race to the Altar': Philip Neri and Ignatius Loyola," in *Symbol and Image in Iberian Arts*, ed. Margaret A. Rees (Leeds: Trinity and All Saints College, 1994), 151-60.

52. For the letter, see *The Letters and Instructions of Francis Xavier*, trans. M. Joseph Costelloe (St. Louis: Institute of Jesuit Sources, 1992), 63-74.

53. See Costelloe, *Letters and Instructions*, xxiii-xxiv.

54. See *For Matters of Greater Moment: The First Thirty Jesuit General Congregations. A Brief History and a Translation of the Decrees*, ed. John W. Padberg, et al. (St. Louis: Institute of Jesuit Sources, 1994), 212, decree 71; ibid., 218, decree 3.

55. Horatius Torsellinus [Orazio Torsellino, Torsellini], *De vita Francisci Xaverii . . . quibus accesserunt eiusdem Xaverii epistolarum libri quatuor* (Rome: Luigi Zannetti, 1596). The same year with the same publisher he brought forth separately a Latin translation of the letters

56. See Wright, "'Race,'" 153-55, and König-Nordhoff, *Ignatius*, 41-42.

57. See FN 3:428, as well as Louis Ponnelle and Louis Bordet, *St. Philip Neri and the Roman Society of His Times* (1515-95), trans. Ralph Francis Kerr (London: Sheed and Ward, 1932), 99-105, especially 101.

58. Pedro de Ribadeneyra, *Flos sanctorum, o Libro de las vidas de los Santos*, 2 vols. (Madrid: Luis Sanchez, 1599-1601), 2:872, my translation.

59. See FN 4:931.

60. See *Flos sanctorum*, 2:846.

61. See ibid., 2:843.

62. Javier Azpeitia ventures a much larger pagination estimate in a modern edition of a few selections from the *Flor sanctorum: Pedro de Ribadeneyra, Vidas de santos; Antología del Flos sanctorum*, eds. Olalla Aguirre and Javier Azpetia (Madrid: Ediciones Lengua de Trapo, 2000), xxxii.

63. For the printing history, see Carlos Sommervogel, et al., *Bibliothèque de la Compagnie de Jésus*, 12 vols. (Brussels, Paris, Toulouse, 1890-1932), 6:1738-1754.

64. The most extensive account of this quest and related matters is of course König-Nordhoff, *Ignatius*. See also, however, Alfonso Rodríguez Gutiérrez de Ceballos, "La iconografía de San Ignacio de Loyola y los ciclos pintados de su vida en España e Hispanoamérica," in Plazaola, *Ignacio y su tiempo*, 107-28; Heinrich Pfeiffer, "The Iconography of the Society of Jesus," in *The Jesuits and the Arts, 1540-1773*, ed. John W. O'Malley and Gauvin Alexander Bailey (Philadelphia: Saint Joseph's University Press, 2003), 201-28, at 206-11; and Pierre-Antoine Fabre, "Les voies d'une canonisation: Écriture, portrait et récit de vie dans l'invention flamande de saint Ignace de Loyola," in *Confessional Sanctity* (c. 1500—c. 1800, ed. Jürgen Beyer, et al. (Mainz: Philipp von Zabern, 2003), 133-48.

65. See König-Nordhoff, *Ignatius*, 261-65.

66. See ibid., 109-14, and image # 270.

67. See ibid., 101-9, and image #283, as well as Michael Bury, *The Print in Italy 1550-1620* (London: British Museum Press, 2001), 131. I am indebted to Simon Ditchfield for the reference to Bury.

68. On Wilhelm and the Jesuits, see Jeffrey Chipps Smith, *Sensuous Worship: Jesuits and the Art of the Early Catholic Reformation in Germany* (Princeton: Princeton University Press, 2002), especially 57-75.

69. König-Nordhoff has transcribed the letter, *Ignatius*, 189, n. 806.

70. The *Chronicon*, originally intended for Mercurian to help him in his governance of the Society, was not published until the late nineteenth century: Juan Alfonso de Polanco, *Vita Ignatii Loiolae et rerum Societatis Iesu historia*, 6 vols. (Madrid: Typographorum Societas [vol. 1] and Avrial [vols. 2-6], 1894-98). Polanco's principal source was the incoming correspondence of the Jesuit curia for those years.

71. FN 1:136-38.

72. Ibid., 1:194.

73. Ibid., 1:496-97 (#95).

74. Ibid., 4:260-61.

75. Ibid., 4:925.

76. Ibid., 1:402-3 (#29).

77. Ibid., 4:125.

78. See O'Malley and Bailey, *Jesuits and the Arts*, 46-47.

79. FN 4:636-59.

80. See ibid., 4:356-58. See also the entry, "Acquaviva [sic], Rodolfo," in O'Neill, *Diccionario*, 1:12-13, and Gauvin Alexander Bailey, *Art on the Jesuit Missions in Asia and Latin America, 1542-1773* (Toronto: University of Toronto Press, 1999), 112-18.

81. See FN 4:358-59. See also the entry, "Azevado (Acevado), Ignacio de," in O'Neill, *Diccionario*, 1:313.

82. See the entry, "Martínez, Pedro," ibid., 3:2524.

83. See FN 4:356-57. See also the entry, "Seguar, Juan Bautista de," in O'Neill, *Diccionario*, 4:3549-3550, and Clifford M. Lewis and Albert J. Loomie, *The Spanish Jesuit Mission in Virginia, 1570-1572* (Chapel Hill: University of North Carolina Press, 1953).

84. See FN 4:356-57, and 480-83. See also the entry, "Criminali (Criminale, Criminal), Antonio (Pietro Antonio)," in O'Neill, *Diccionario*, 2:1000.

85. See FN 4:358-59. See also the entries, "Campion, Edmundo," in O'Neill, *Diccionario* 1:617-618, and "Cottam, Thomas," ibid., 2:984; more generally, see Thomas M. McCoog, *The Reckoned Expense: Edmund Campion and the Early English Jesuits*, 2nd rev. ed. (Rome: Institutum Historicum Societatis Iesu, 2007).

86. See the entry, "Salès, Jacques," in O'Neill, *Diccionario*, 4:3472.

Chronology of Ignatius' Life

1491   Born at the family castle, Loyola, Spain

1521   Wounded in battle at Pamplona

       Recuperates at the castle of Loyola, where his spiritual conversion begins

1522   Makes a pilgrimage to Virgin's shrine at the Benedictine Abbey, Montserrat

       Spends a year at Manresa, outside Barcelona. Makes notes of his religious experiences that will develop into the *Spiritual Exercises*

1523   Sets out for Italy in order to travel as a pilgrim from there to Palestine

       Returns to Spain by way of Italy

1524   Begins study of Latin at Barcelona

       Transfers to the University of Alcalá

       Briefly imprisoned at Alcalá by the Inquisition

1527   Transfers to the University of Salamanca

       After a short while transfers to the University of Paris, where he eventually receives his Master of Arts degree

1534   In Paris on August 15, he and six companions pronounce vows, the nucleus of the future Society of Jesus. They promise to travel together to Palestine

1535   Returns briefly to Loyola from Paris for reasons of health

1536   Travels to Venice to await the companions from Paris

1537   The companions, now nine, arrive in Venice to await passage to Palestine

       Those who were not priests, including Ignatius, are ordained

1539   Gathered in Rome and unable to secure passage to Palestine, the companions decide to found a new religious order

1540   Pope Paul III on September 27 formally approves the Society of Jesus

       Francis Xavier leaves Rome for Portugal where he will take ship for "the Indies" the following year

1541   Ignatius is elected first superior general of the Society

       He begins to write the Jesuit Constitutions

1548   The *Spiritual Exercises* are published in a Latin edition

1556   Ignatius dies in Rome

1609   Ignatius is beatified by Pope Paul V

1622   Ignatius is canonized by Pope Gregory XV along with Francis Xavier, Teresa of Avila, Isidore of Madrid, and Philip Neri

Abbreviations

These abbreviations are used in the following notes.

FN = *Fontes narrativi de S. Ignatio de Loyola et de Societatis Iesu initiis,* ed. Cándido de Dalmases, 4 vols. Monumenta Historica Societatis Iesu 66, 73, 85, 93 (Rome: Monumenta Historica Societatis Iesu, 1943-65)

Ignatius, *Acta* = "Acta Patris Ignatii Scripta a P. Lud. Gonzalez de Camara 1553/1555," in FN 1:323-507

Ribadeneyra, *Flos sanctorum* = Pedro de Ribadeneyra, *Flos sanctorum, o Libro de las vidas de los Santos,* 2 vols. (Madrid: Luis Sanchez, 1599-1601)

Ribadeneyra, *Vida* = Pedro de Ribadeneyra, *Vita Ignatii Loiolae, Textus Latinus et Hispanus cum censuris.* FN 4

Further Reading

Cándido de Dalmases, S. J. *Ignatius of Loyola, Founder of the Society of Jesus: His Life and Work.* Trans. Jerome Aixalá, S.J. St Louis: Institute of Jesuit Sources, 1985.

John W. O'Malley, S.J. *The First Jesuits.* Cambridge, MA: Harvard University Press, 1993.

José Ignacio Tellechea Idígoras. *Ignatius of Loyola: The Pilgrim Saint.* Trans. Cornelius Michael Buckley, S.J. Chicago: Loyola University Press, 1994.

ANNOTATED FACSIMILE

Neither roses nor lilies are lacking among his flowers

[Ignatius]

Blessed
Aloysius
Gonzaga

Blessed
Francis Xavier

Blessed
Stanislaus
Kostka

Blessed
Antonio
Criminali

Blessed Rodolfo Aquaviva
and Companions

Blessed
Edmund
Campion

Blessed
Abraham
Francisco
de
Georgiis

Jesus
[seal of the Society]

The Life of
Blessed Father Ignatius
of Loyola,
Founder of
the Society of Jesus
Rome, 1609

Blessed
Jacques Salès
and
Guillaume
Saultemouche

Many in
England

Many in
India

Forty Martyrs

In Japan

In Florida

The title page (opposite) is translated above and analyzed in detail on pages 27-30.
Neither roses: dactylic hexameter. Lilies represent purity and roses martyrdom.

FLORIBVS EIVS NEC ROSÆ NEC LILIA DESVNT

B. FRANCISC

RVDVLPHVS AQVAVIVA CVM SOCIIS

IH S

VITA
BEATI P. IGNATII
LOIOLÆ
SOCIETATIS IESV
FVNDATORIS.
ROMÆ
M.DC.IX.

QVADRAGINTA MARTYRES

IN IAPONE.

IN FLORIDA

In omni opere dedit confessionem Sancto,
et ab extremis terrae adduxit fratres suos munus Domino.
Ecclesiasticus 47[:9], Isaiah 66[:20]

In every work he gave witness to the Holy One,
and from the ends of the earth
he brought his brothers as a gift to the Lord

[The quotation from Isaiah is approximate,
and seemingly composite of 66:20, 41:9, and 43:6.]

IHS

In omni opere dedit confessionem Sancto, et ab extremis
terræ adduxit fratres suos
munus Domino.
Eccl. 47.   Isa. 66.

1

Mater Ignatium paritura pro sua in na-
talem Domini pietate deferri se iubet in
stabulum; eumque post septem filios postre-
mum in stabulo parit, an. salutis 1491

His mother, about to give birth to Ignatius,
because of her devotion to the Lord's nativity,
orders that she be brought into the stable,
and in a stable gives birth to him,
coming after seven sons,
in the year of salvation 1491.

The mention of Ignatius as the last of eight brothers recalls 1 Sam 16:1-10; thus Ignatius is likened not only to Jesus—born in a stable—but to King David!

Mater Ignatium paritura pro sua in na-
talem Domini pietate, deferri se iubet in
stabulum; eumq; post septem filios postre-
mum in stabulo parit, anº. salutis. 1 4 9 1.

.1.

2

Militiam sequutus Ignatius ictu muralis
globi crure perfracto a defensione arcis
Pampelonae semianimis excutitur ut secu-
lari militia relicta ad divinam se transferat.

Pursuing a military career,
Ignatius is driven from the defense of the fort at Pamplona, half-dead,
when a cannon ball strikes the wall and his leg is broken,
so that, the worldly army left behind, ·
he might betake himself to God's.

---

worldly army, God's army: the same conceit is found in no. 11.

Ignatius, *Acta* (#1-2), FN 1:364-367

Ribadeneyra, *Vida*, FN 4:80-83

Militiam sequutus Ignatius, ictu muralis
globi crure perfracto à defensione arcis
Pampelonæ semianimis excutitur vt secu-
lari militia relicta, ad diuinam se transferat.

2

3

*E cruris vulnere laboranti mortique iam
proximo S. Petrus in sui pervigilij nocte
per quietem apparet ac sanitatem restituit.*

As he is suffering from the wound to his leg, and near death,
St. Peter appears to him as he sleeps,
during the night of the vigil of his feast,
and restores his health.

Ignatius, *Acta* (#3), FN 1: 366-369

Ribadeneyra, *Vida,* FN 4:82-85

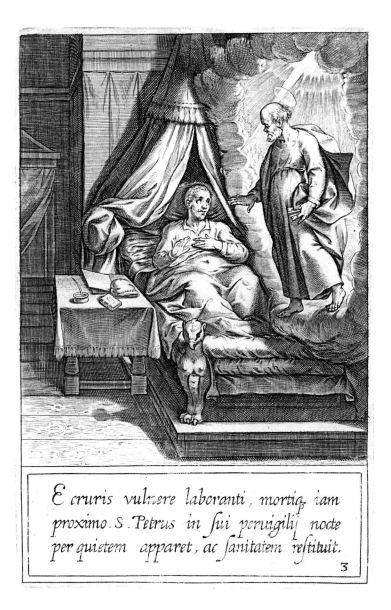

E cruris vulnere laboranti, mortiꝗ iam
proximo. S. Petrus in sui peruigilij nocte
per quietem apparet, ac sanitatem restituit.

3

4

*In lecto decumbens, dum ad recreandum
animum Christi domini vitam et exempla Sanctorum evolvit, divinarum virtutum
imitatione exardescens ad Deum convertitur.*

Lying in bed, while to restore his spirits
he opens up a Life of Christ our Lord
and books of *exempla* of the saints,
becoming inflamed with the desire to imitate such divine virtues,
he undergoes a conversion to God.

Ignatius, *Acta* (#5-9), FN 1:368-375

Ribadeneyra, *Vida*, FN 4:86-91

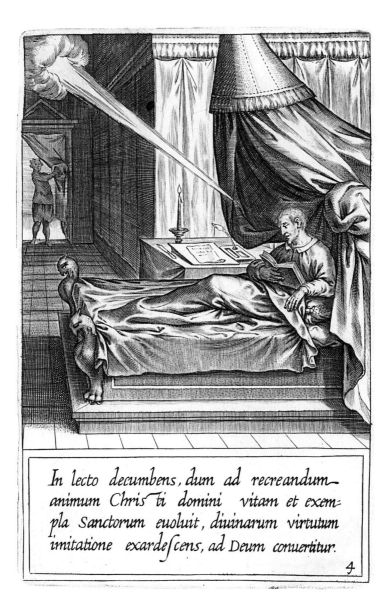

In lecto decumbens, dum ad recreandum
animum Chris ti domini vitam et exempla Sanctorum euoluit, diuinarum virtutum
imitatione exarde/cens, ad Deum conuertitur.

4

5

Dum se invocata divinae Matris ope Deo
dicat noctu vigilantem Beatiss. Virgo eiusque
in gremio puer Iesus illustri in specie
aliquandiu visi suavissime recreant.

As he dedicates himself to God
invoking the help of the Mother of God, and keeps night vigil,
the Most Blessed Virgin and the Child Jesus in her lap,
seen for some time in bright appearance,
provide sweetest comfort.

Ignatius, *Acta* (#10), FN 1:374-377

Ribadeneyra, *Vida*, FN 4:90-93

Dum se invocata divinæ Matris ope Deo
dicat noctu vigilantem Beatiss. Virgo eiusq̃
in gremio puer Iesus illustri in specie
aliquandiu visi suauissime recreant.

5

6

Dum se Deo iterum fusus in preces
ferventissime offert, magno repente
terrae motu concutitur domus.

As he again offers himself to God
most fervently pouring himself out in prayer,
suddenly the house is shaken by a great earthquake.

Suddenly . . . earthquake: perhaps reminiscences of Matt 28:2, et ecce terraemotus factus est magnus, and Acts 2:2, et factus est repente de caelo sonus tamquam advenientis spiritus vehementis

Ribadeneyra, *Vida,* FN 4:90-93

Dum se Deo iterum fusus in preces
feruentissime offert, magno repente
terræ motu concutitur domus.

6

7

*E domo et cognatione sua exit rectaque
ad Virginis templum famulis redire
iussis, in Montem Serratum contendit. (50, 62)*

He leaves home and kindred,
and ordering his servants to return
he hastens straightway to the Virgin's shrine, Montserrat.

Home and kindred: Gen 12:1, Egredere de terra tua et de cognatione tua et de domo patris tui

Ignatius, *Acta* (#12), FN 1:376-379

Ribadeneyra, *Vida*, FN 4:96-99

E domo & cognatione sua exit, rectaque
ad Virginis templum famulis redire-
iussis, in Montem Serratum contendit.

7

8

In itinere Maurum de virginitate Dei matris
impure detrahentem dubitat an ferro ulciscatur,
permissisque equo habenis, ex eo quod iumentum ab
antecedentis Mauri vestigijs divertit, divinitus in-
terpretatur huiusmodi ultionem Deo cordi non esse.

On his journey, a Moor indecently detracted from the
virginity of the Mother of God, and he doubts whether or no
he should avenge himself by the sword on him;
but when he gives the reins over to the mule,
because the beast turns away from the tracks of the path
the Moor had taken, by divine inspiration he realizes that
this kind of vengeance is not after God's heart.

God's heart: 1 Sam 14:13; cf. 1 Sam 24:13

Ignatius, *Acta* (#15-16), FN 1:382-387

Ribadeneyra, *Vida*, FN 4:100-103

In itinere Maurum de virginitate Dei matris
impure detrahentem dubitat an ferro vlciscatur,
permißisq; equo habenis, ex eo quòd iumentum ab
antecedentis Mauri vestigijs diuertit, diuinitus in=
terpretatur huiusmodi vltionem Deo cordi non eße.

8

9

In eodem itinere B. Virginis amore atque
imitatione succensus voto se illi castitatis
obstringit; eiusdemque castitatis, omni extincto
impuritatis sensu, perpetuum donum accipit.

On the same journey, inflamed with a desire to love
and imitate the Blessed Virgin, he binds himself to her
by a vow of chastity, and with all impure feelings quenched
he receives that same chastity as a lifelong gift.

Ignatius, *Acta* (#10), FN 1:374-377

Ribadeneyra, *Vida*, FN 4:102-103

In eodem itinere, B. Virginis amore, atque
imitatione succensus voto se illi castitatis
obstringit; eiusdemq; castitatis, omni extincto
impuritatis sensu, perpetuum donum accipit.

9

10

Vestibus pretiosis exutus, ac pauperi
donatis, sacco ac fune praecinctus
Christi domini paupertatem amplectitur.

Taking off his costly garments
and giving them to a poor man,
girding himself with sackcloth and rope,
he embraces the poverty of Christ our Lord.

Ignatius, *Acta* (#18), FN 1:386-389

Ribadeneyra, *Vida*, FN 4:104-107

Vestibus pretiosis exutus, ac pauperi donatis, sacco ac fune præcinctus Christi domini paupertatem amplectitur.

10

11

In Aede Montis Serrati tamquam novus
Christi eques noctem unam ante aram
Virginis excubat, humanaeque arma
militiae e tholo suspendit.

In the shrine of Montserrat, as a new knight of Christ,
he keeps watch one entire night before the altar of the Virgin
and hangs the weapon of a human army from the dome.

From the dome: cf. Aeneid 9.408

Ignatius, *Acta* (#17), FN 1:386-387

Ribadeneyra, *Vida*, FN 4:104-105

In Æde Montis Serrati tamquam nouus
Christi eques noctem vnam ante aram
Virginis excubat, humanæque arma
militiæ e tholo suspendit.

12

In solitudinem profectus, furente supra oran-
tis caput varijs serpentum spectris daemone
intrepidus atque inconnivens in precibus perseverat.

Going forth into solitude,
though the demon rages in various visions
of serpents over his head as he prays,
in prayer he perseveres unflinching and unblinking.

Ignatius, *Acta* (#19), FN 1:388-391

Ribadeneyra, *Vida*, FN 4:126-127

In solitudinem profectus, furente supra oran-
tis caput uarijs serpentum spectris dæmone
intrepidus atq̃ inconniuens in precibus perseuerat.

12

13

Minoressae inter pauperum turbam vivit,
xenodochio inservit, multos e vitiorum
coeno extrahit.

At Manresa he lives among a crowd of poor men,
serves in the strangers' hospice,
draws many from the filth of vices.

This was the hospice of Santa Lucía in Manresa.

Ignatius, Acta (#18-19), FN 1:388-391

Ribadeneyra, *Vida*, FN 4:108-111

Minoreſſæ inter pauperum turbam viuit,
xenodochio inſeruit, multos e vitiorum
coeno extrahit.

13

14

Horas quotidie septenas genibus nixus
in oratione persistit. Quotidie etiam ter
sese quam acerrime flagellis caedit.

Seven hours every day on his knees
he continues steadfastly in prayer.
Every day also he thrice beats himself
with most severe flagellation.

Ignatius, *Acta* (#23), FN 1:394-397

Ribadeneyra, *Vida*, FN 4:108-109

Horas quotidie septenas genibus nixus
in oratione persis tit. Quotidie etiam ter
sese quam acerrime flagellis cædit.

14

15

Quotidie aqua et pane contentus severe
ieiunat, imo ad evincendos scrupulos, quorum
angustijs a daemone ad praecipitium usque
instigabatur; septem dies sine ullo cibo
aut potu, nullo virium defectu transigit.

Every day, content with bread and water,
he gives himself to strict fasting;
indeed, to overcome scruples,
by whose torments he was driven by a demon
even to throw himself headlong,
he spends seven days without any food or drink
with no diminishment of strength.

Ignatius, *Acta* (#22-24), FN 1:392-397

Ribadeneyra, *Vida*, FN 4:108-121

Quotidie aqua et pane contentus seuere
ieiunat, imo ad euincendos scrupulos, quorum
angustijs a dæmone ad præcipitium vsque
instigabatur, septem dies sine vllo cibo
aut potu, nullo virium defectu transigit.

95

16

Dum apud templi dominicani limina Beatae
Virginis laudes recitat, miram de sanctissimo
Trinitatis mysterio visionem et lumina accipit.

At the threshold of the Dominican church
as he recites Lauds of the Office of the Blessed Virgin,
he receives a wonderful vision and illumination
about the most holy mystery of the Trinity.

Ignatius, *Acta* (#28), FN 1:400-403

Ribadeneyra, *Vida*, FN 4:120-123

Dum apud templi dominicani limina Beatæ
Virgini laudes recitat, miram de sanctißimo
Trinitatis mysterio visionem, et lumina accipit.

16

17

Eodem in templo dum missae sacri-
ficio interest in sacrosancta hostia
Christum D[omi]num oculis intuetur.

In the same church,
while he is present at the sacrifice of the Mass,
in the most sacred Host he beholds
Christ our Lord with his own eyes.

Ignatius, *Acta* (#29), FN 1:402-403

Ribadeneyra, *Vida*, FN 4:124-125

Eodem in templo dum missæ sacri-
ficio interest in sacrosancta hostia
Christum Dñum oculis intuetur.

17

18

Saepe Christus dominus eiusque Mater ei ad lon-
gum temporis spatium contemplandos fruendosque
se exhibent, magnamque eius animo inspirant in
christiana fide atque in suscepta pietate constantiam.

Often Christ our Lord and his mother
show themselves to him for long periods of time
to be contemplated and enjoyed,
and inspire within his spirit great constancy in Christian faith
and in the life of devotion he has undertaken.

Ignatius, *Acta* (#29), FN 1:402-405

Ribadeneyra, *Vida*, FN 4:124-125

Sæpe Christus dominus, eiusq; Mater ei ad lon-
gum temporis spatium, contemplandos fruendosq;
se exhibent; magnamq; eius animo inspirant in
christiana fide, atq; in suscepta pietate constantiam.

98

19

In mentis raptu septem ipsos dies persisten-
tem humaturi iam erant, nisi e tenuissima
cordis palpitatione vitae indicium deprehendissent,
a quo tandem raptu veluti a dulci somno
nomen IESU suaviter ingeminans solvitur.

As he continued in a swoon for those seven days,
they would have buried him had they not detected
a sign of life from a slight beating of the heart;
from which swoon finally, as from a sweet sleep,
gently repeating the name of Jesus he is released.

Ribadeneyra, *Vida*, FN 4:128129

In mentis raptu septem ipsos dies persisten-
tem humaturi iam erant, nisi e tenuissima
cordis palpitatione vitæ indicium deprehendissent;
a quo tandem raptu veluti a dulci somno,
nomen IESV suauiter ingeminans soluitur.

19

20

*Magnam divinarum humanarumque
rerum cognitionem divinitus
infusam accipit.*

He receives great understanding of things
both human and divine,
divinely infused.

Ignatius, *Acta* (#28-31), FN 1:400-407

Ribadeneyra, *Vida*, FN 4:126-127

Magnam diuinarum humanarumq;
rerum cognitionem diuinitus
infusam accipit.

20

21

Libellum exercitiorum spiritualium sin-
gulari afflatu Dei haustaque e
coelo luce conscribit.

He writes the book of Spiritual Exercises,
by a special inspiration
of God and by light drawn from heaven.

Ribadeneyra, *Vida*, FN 4:134-141

Libellum exercitiorum spiritualium sin-
gulari afflatu Dei, haustaque e
cælo luce conscribit.

21

22

Navigaturus in Italiam sola DEI
fiducia pro viatico munitus emen-
dicatam pecuniam in littus abjicit.

About to sail to Italy,
protected by trust in God alone
as his provision for the journey,
he throws away onto the shore
the money he has begged.

Ignatius, *Acta* (#36-37), FN 1:410-413
Ribadeneyra, *Vida*, FN 4:146-147

Nauigaturus in Italiam sola DEI
fiducia pro uiatico munitus emen-
dicatam pecuniam in littus abijcit.

22

23

Prope Patavium viae noctis et tempo-
rum periculis anxium, apparens in
aere Christus Dominus consolatur.

Near Padua, as he is anxious about the journey
because of dangers at night and the weather,
Christ our Lord appears in the air and consoles him.

---

in the air: 1 Thess 4:17, simul rapiemur cum illis in nubibus obviam Domino in aera

Ignatius, Acta (#41), FN 1:416-419

Ribadeneyra, *Vida,* FN 4:124-125

Prope Patauium viæ noctis et tempo=
rum periculis anxium, apparens in
aëre Christus Dominus consolatur.

23

24

Venetijs dum noctu sub S. Marci porticibus
iacet, M. Antonius Trevisanus nobilis Senator
hisce verbis excitatus: Tu delicate quidem cubas
sed famulus interim meus humi sub dio est, ho-
minem sedulo quaerit ac suscipit perhumaniter.

In Venice, at night, while he lies in the porticos of St. Mark's,
M[arco] Antonio Trevisano, a noble senator, was awakened
by these words: "You repose in luxury indeed
but meanwhile my servant is on the ground in the open air."
He solicitously seeks out and takes care of the man with great kindness."

---

on the ground . . . men . . . kindness: in the Latin, puns on *humi* and *hominem* and *perhumaniter*

Ignatius, *Acta* (#42), FN 1:418-419

Ribadeneyra, *Vida*, FN 4:152-155

Venetijs dum noctu ſub S. Marci porticibus
iacet, M. Antonius Treuiſanus nobilis Senator
hiſce verbis excitatus Tu delicate quidem cubas,
sed famulus interim meus humi ſub dio eſt, hominem ſedulo quærit ac ſuscipit perhumaniter.

24

25

Nautae suis infensum vitijs in deser-
tam Insulam exposituri, subito vento re-
pelluntur, ac inviti licet ad Cyprum vehunt.

Because he was hostile to their vices,
the sailors were going to set him ashore on a desert island,
but are driven back by a sudden wind and,
however unwilling, carry him to Cyprus.

Cf. Jonah 1:7-15

Ignatius, *Acta* (#43-44), FN 1:418-423

Ribadeneyra, *Vida*, FN 4:154-155

Nautæ suis infensum vitijs in deser=
tam Insulam exposituri, subito vento re=
pelluntur, ac inuiti licet ad Cyprum uehunt.

25

26

*Hierosolymam naviganti saepe Christus
dominus videndum se praebet ac labo-
rum difficultates lenit.*

As he sails to Jerusalem Christ our Lord
often shows himself and lightens
the hardships he undergoes.

Ignatius, *Acta* (#44), FN 1:420-423

Ribadeneyra, *Vida*, FN 4:154-155

Hierosolymam nauiganti sæpe Christus
dominus videndum se præbet, ac labo=
rum difficultates lenit.

26

27

*Sacra Palestinae loca religiosissime perlustrat
et ad montem Olivetum Christi Domi-
ni ascendentis vestigia diligentius con-
templaturus eum capitis periculo recurrit.*

He most devoutly tours all through the holy places of Palestine,
and to contemplate more thoroughly the footprints
of Christ our Lord when he ascended, he keeps going back
to the Mount of Olives, at mortal peril to himself.

Ignatius, *Acta* (#47), FN 1:426-427

Ribadeneyra, *Vida,* FN 4:158-161

Sacra Palestinæ loca religiosissimè perlustrat,
et ad montem Oliuetum Christi Domi=
ni ascendentis uestigia diligentius con-
templaturus cum capitis periculo recurrit.

27

28

Ex Oliveto revertens ab Armenio custode voce
ac fuste terretur; dumque ne solitarius ea loca pera-
graret, ferociter in hospitium trahitur, inter ea con-
vicia et contumelias Christum aspicit praeeuntem.

Coming back from Olivet he is frightened by the Armenian guardian,
by his voice and staff, and while, lest he wander through those places
all by himself, he is dragged roughly to a hospice amid reproaches
and contumely, he sees Christ going before him.

Ignatius, *Acta* (#48), FN 1:426-427

Ribadeneyra, *Vida*, FN 4:16-161

Ex Oliueto reuertens ab Armenio custode voce,
ac fuste terretur; dumq̃ ne solitarius ea loca pera-
graret, ferociter in hospitium trahitur, inter ea con-
uicia, et contumelias Christum aspicit praeeuntem.

28

29

In Hispaniam rediturum a navi Veneta optime in-
structa Nauarchus excludit respondetque sanctitatem viri
extollentibus: Si sanctus est quid navim petit, ac
mare sicco vestigio non alcat. Quare in aliam re-
lictam ac laceram admittitur; sed haec incolumis in His-
paniam appellit, Veneta quamvis valida naufragium facit.

As he prepares to return to Spain
the captain of a very well outfitted Venetian ship
turns him away and replies to those extolling the man's sanctity:
"If he is a saint, why is he looking for a ship?
Why doesn't he walk upon the sea dryshod?"
So he is taken aboard another ship, one abandoned and full of holes;
but it makes for Spain safe and sound,
while the Venetian one, though fit, suffers shipwreck.

The caption is misleading. Although Ignatius was ultimately headed for Spain, he had to go there by way of Italy. His ship landed at a port in Apulia, probably Bari.

dryshod: cf. Exod 14:22, et ingressi sunt filii Israhel per medium maris sicci; and Josh 4:18, et siccam humum calcare coepissent

Ignatius, *Acta* (#49), FN 1:428-431

Ribadeneyra, *Vida*, FN 4:158-163

In Hispaniam rediturum a naui Veneta optime in-
structa Nauarchus excludit, respondetq́ sanctitatem viri
extollentibus. Si sanctus est quid nauim petit, ac
mare sicco vestigio non calcat? Quare in aliam re-
lictam ac laceram admittitur. Sed hæc incolumis in Hispaniam appellit Veneta quamuis valida naufragiũ facit.

29

30

Pecuniam in summo Ferrariae Templo peten-
tibus ab se pauperibus elargitur, cogitumque eo die
ostiatim pro se victum emendicare; quo observa-
to a pauperibus Sanctus palam conclamatur.

In the cathedral church of Ferrara,
when the poor ask him for money he gives it out;
on that same day, when he is forced to beg food for himself
door to door and the poor men note this,
he is openly acclaimed a saint.

Ignatius, *Acta* (#50), FN 1:430-431

Ribadeneyra, *Vida*, FN 4:162-165

Pecuniam in summo Ferrariæ Templo peten-
tibus ab se pauperibus elargitur; cogitur eo die
ostiatim pro se victum emendicare; quo obserua-
to a pauperibus, Sanctus palam conclamatur.

30

31

Ab Hispanorum praesidio pro exploratore
habitus nudus per media castra raptatur
quam ignominiam alacriter ferenti, species
oblata est Christi domini ad Herodem
a Pilato transmissi atque illusi.

From a Spanish fortress, taken for a spy,
he is dragged naked through the middle of the camp;
as he readily bears the shame,
the image is offered him of Christ our Lord
sent over from Pilate to Herod, and mocked.

At this time Spanish troops were in Lombardy, northern Italy, fighting against the French for possession of the duchy of Milan.

Ignatius, *Acta* (#51-52), FN 1:430-433

Ribadeneyra, *Vida*, FN 4:164-167

Ab Hispanorum præsidio pro exploratore
habitus nudus per media castra raptatur.
quam ignominiam alacriter ferenti, species
oblata est Christi domini ad Herodem
a Pilato transmissi, atque illusi.

31

32

Barcinone ut se ad animorum salutem instruat
prima Grammaticae elementa annos tres et tri-
ginta natus addiscit, furente ac rumpente se
Daemone, qui importunis rerum caelestium gau-
dijs avocare alio eius animum frustra conatur.

In Barcelona that he might equip himself
for the salvation of souls, at thirty-three years of age
he learns the first elements of grammar;
a demon rages and rends himself, and strives in vain
to divert his spirit elsewhere, to distracting joys of heavenly things.

Ignatius, *Acta* (#54-55), FN 1:434-438

Ribadeneyra, *Vida,* FN 168-173

Barcinone vt se ad animorum salutem instruat
prima Grammaticæ elementa annos tres, et tri=
ginta natus addiscit; furente ac rumpente se
Dæmone, qui importunis rerum cælestium gau=
dijs auocare alio eius animum frustra conatur.

32

33

Ob restitutam in virginum coenobio
disciplinam ab impuris hominibus id indig-
ne ferentibus saevissime plagis afficitur.

Because he restored proper discipline in a convent of virgins,
lecherous men who found it intolerable
afflict him with most savage blows.

Ribadeneyra, *Flos sanctorum,* 2:814

Ob res titutam in virginum coenobio
disciplinam ab impuris hominibus id indig:
ne ferentibus sæuissime plagis afficitur.

33

34

Hominem ad suspendium desperatione coactum
precibus ad sensus eatenus revocat, quoad
animum a scelere Confessionis sacramento purget.

When hopelessness drove a man to the point of hanging himself,
by his prayers he calls him back to his senses
to such an extent that by the sacrament of Confession
he purges his spirit from wickedness.

Ribadeneyra, *Flos sanctorum,* 2:814

Hominem ad suspendium desperatione coactum
precibus ad sensus eatenus reuocat, quoad
animum a scelere, Confessionis sacramento purget.

34

35

Noctu fusus in preces quatuor ferme cubitis
elatus a terra, collucente mirum in modum
facie identidem crebra inter suspiria inclamat,
O DOMINE SI TE HOMINES NOSSENT!

At night pouring himself out in prayer,
lifted from up the earth almost four cubits,
his face lit up in marvelous wise,
again and again with many sighs he cries,
"O Lord, if only men knew you!"

Juan Pasqual, "Narratio prior" (1579), FN 3:142-151, at 149

*Noctu fusus in preces, quatuor ferme cubitis
elatus a terra, collucente mirum in modum
facie, identidem, crebra inter suspiria inclamat.*
O DOMINE SI TE HOMINES NOSSENT!

35

36

Compluti primum, postea Salmanticae, calumnias
pro Christo et carcerem passus, ex ipso etiam car-
cere animas lucratur magnoque spiritus fervore
succensus. Non tot inquit in hac urbe sunt com-
pedes quin plures ego Christi causa percupiam.

First at Alcalá, afterwards at Salamanca,
having suffered calumnies and imprisonment for Christ,
from that same prison he gains souls
and is inflamed with great fervor of spirit.
He says, "There are not so many shackles in this city
that I would not desire still more for the sake of Christ."

Ignatius, *Acta* (#58-62, 65-70), FN 1:442-451, 454-463

Ribadeneyra, *Vida*, FN 4:178-197

Compluti primum ; postea Salmanticæ, calumnias
pro Christo, et carcerem passus, ex ipso etiam car-
cere animas lucratur, magnoq̃ spiritus feruore
succensus. Non tot, inquit, in hac vrbe sunt com-
pedes, quin plures ego Christi causa percupiam.

37

Quidam ei infensus imprecans sibi aliquando
flammas, quibus combustus expiraret, nisi
Ignatius ignem se iudice mereretur, eodem die
incendio domus suae deflagrantis absumptus est.

A certain man, hostile to him, called down fire upon himself:
he said that if Ignatius (as he saw it) did not deserve the flames,
he himself should catch on fire and perish.
That same day his house went up in flames;
and he was himself consumed.

Ribadeneyra, *Flos sanctorum*, 2:816

Quidam ei infensus imprecans sibi aliquando
Flammas, quibus combustus expiraret, nisi
Ignatius ignem se iudice mereretur, eodem die
incendio domus suæ deflagrantis absumptus est.

37

38

Dum Luteriae tamquam scholasticorum seductor
virgis in publica animadversione caedendus
inducitur, cognita hominis innocentia Rector
ad eius pedes accidit, sanctum palam appellat,
infamiaeque apparatum in gloriae scenam vertit.

As he is brought in to be beaten with rods, in a public censure,
as one who leads the students astray towards Lutheranism,
the Rector, realizing the man's innocence, falls at his feet,
openly calls him a saint, and turns an occasion of disgrace
into a scene of glory.

The rector was Diogo de Gouveia of the College of Sainte-Barbe, Paris, who became an influential friend of the Jesuits.

Ignatius, *Acta* (#78), FN 1:468-471

Ribadeneyra, *Vida*, FN 4:220-227

Dum Luteriæ tamquam scholasticorum seductor
virgis in publica animaduersione cædendus
inducitur, cognita hominis innocentia Rector
ad eius pedes accidit, sanctum palam appellat,
infamiæ apparatum in gloriæ scenam vertit.

38

39

Iuvenes ex Academia Parisiensi novem
eligit ac socios consilij sui destinat.

He chooses nine young men from the University of Paris
and makes them companions in his plans.

Ignatius, *Acta* (#82, 85), FN 1:474-477, 478-481

Ribadeneyra, *Vida,* FN 4:228-231

Iuuenes ex Academia Parisiensi nouem
eligit, ac socios consilij sui des tinat.

39

40

Sicarius stricto illum ferro petens, audita
repente voce QUO TENDIS INFELIX?
territus a facinore desistit.

A murderer rushes at him with drawn sword
when suddenly a voice is heard,
"Where are you going, wretch?";
frightened he desists from crime.

Ribadeneyra, *Vida*, FN 4:766-767

Sicarius stricto illum ferro petens, audita
repente voce QVO TENDIS INFELIX?
territus a facinore desistit.

40

41

*In aede suburbana B. Virginis ipse ac socij certo se
voto obstringunt divinam ubique gloriam animarumque
salutem in Hierosolymitana praesertim expeditione pro-
curandi ac palmam inde martyrij sedulo conqui-
rendi, quod votum ibidem quotannis renovant.*

In a shrine of the Blessed Virgin on the outskirts of the city,
he and his companions bind themselves by a firm vow
to further the glory of God and the salvation of souls everywhere,
especially by a journey to Jerusalem, and thus zealously to attain the
martyr's palm—a vow they renew on the same date every year.

Ignatius, *Acta* (#85), FN 1:478-481

Ribadeneyra, *Vida*, FN 4:232-235

In æde suburbana B Virginis ipse, ac socij certo se
voto obstringunt diuinam vbique gloriam, animarúq̃
salutem in Hierosolymitana præsertim expeditione pro-
curandi, ac palmam inde martyrij sedulo conqui=
rendi, quod votum ibidem quotannis renouant.

49

42

Ab impuris amoribus quempiam revocaturus,
in summa hyeme, gelido se in stagno collo tenus
immergit ibique praetereuntem conspicatus
voce aspectuque terret et convertit.

To call someone away from impure loves, in the depth of winter
he immerses himself up to his neck in a frozen pool,
and there catching sight of the man as he goes by
he puts fear into him by voice and look, and converts him.

Ribadeneyra, *Vida*, FN 4:758-759

Ab impuris amoribus quempiam reuocaturus,
in summa hyeme, gelido se in stagno collo tenus
immergit, ibique prætereuntem conspicatus,
voce, aspectuque terret, et conuertit.

42

43

In Hispaniam valetudinis causa redeuntem,
excitata sanctitatis viri fama armati primum
homines mox clerus omnis agmine composito
demum populus fere universus ingenti gratu-
latione suscipiunt.

As he returns to Spain for his health,
the report of the man's sanctity is bruited about,
and soldiers first, then soon after all the clergy
lined up in procession, and finally virtually the entire populace,
with great rejoicing, welcome him.

Ignatius, *Acta* (#87-89), FN 1:482-487

Ribadeneyra, *Vida*, FN 4:236-237

In Hispaniam valetudinis causa redeuntem
excitata sanctitatis viri fama armati primum
homines mox clerus omnis agmine composito
demum populus fere vniuersus ingenti gratu:
latione suscipiunt.

43

44

Aeger Hispaniam repetens animis ad virtutem
excolendis strenue in patria laborat eiusque in
campo concionantis vox (quod populi frequentiam
templa non caperent) ad trecentos passus auditur.

Ill, returning to Spain, he works energetically
at stimulating souls to virtue,
and his voice as he preaches in the field
(because churches could not accommodate the crowds)
is heard from three hundred feet.

Ignatius, *Acta* (#88), FN 1:482-485

Ribadeneyra, *Vida*, FN 4:236-239

Æger Hispaniam repetens, animis ad virtutem
excolendis strenue in patria laborat; eiusq; in
campo concionantis vox (quod populi frequentiam
templa non caperent) ad trecentos passus auditur.

44

45

Comitiali morbo laborantem sublatis in
coelum oculis, ac precibus extemplo sanat.

Lifting up his eyes to heaven and praying,
he immediately heals a man stricken by epilepsy.

Lifting up his eyes: Luke 6:20; John 11:41; 17:1

Ribadeneyra, *Flos sanctorum*, 2:820

Comitiali morbo laborantem sublatis in
coelum oculis, ac precibus extemplo sanat.

45

46

Multos saepe Energumenos liberat
crucis signo.

Often he frees many possessed persons
by the sign of the cross.

Ribadeneyra, *Flos sanctorum,* 2:820

Multos sæpe Energumenos liberat
crucis signo.

46

47

Foeminam phtysi ad interitum pro-
perantem sanitati restituit.

A woman hastening to death from consumption
he restores to health.

Ribadeneyra, *Flos sanctorum*, 2:820

Foeminam phtysi ad interitum pro=
perantem sanitati res tituit.

47

48

Arido emortuoque foeminae bracchio
Ignatij lintea dum lavat vita statim
ac motus redit.

As a woman washes Ignatius's garments,
life and movement immediately return
to her withered and lifeless arm.

Arido, emortuoque foeminæ bracchio
Ignatij lintea dum lauat, vita statim,
ac motus redit.

48.

49

In Italiam reversus Venetiis socios e Gallia
excipit unaque cum illis sacerdotio initiatur tam
coelesti voluptate perfuso Episcopo, ut non nisi
divinum quid in novis sacerdotibus praesagiret.

Returning to Italy,
at Venice he welcomes the companions from France,
and together with them is inducted into the priesthood;
the [ordaining] bishop was so filled with heavenly delight
that he foresaw in these new priests naught but something divine.

Ignatius, *Acta* (#93), FN 1:492-493

Ribadeneyra, *Vida*, FN 4:254-255

In Italiam reuerſus Venetijs ſocios e Gallia
excipit, vnaꝗ cum illis Sacerdotio initiatur, tam
coelesti voluptate perfuso Epiſcopo, vt non niſi
diuinum quid in nouis Sacerdotibus præſagiret.

49

50

Ad Simonem Rodericum socium morti proxi-
mum octodecim milliarium itinere febri ipse
laborans propere contendit, eumque amplexu sanat.

His companion Simâo Rodrigues was close to death,
but though he himself was suffering from a fever,
he quickly hastens to make a journey of eighteen Roman miles,
and heals him with an embrace.

Simâo Rodrigues was one of the original companions of Paris and a founder of the Society.

Ignatius, *Acta* (#95), FN 1:494-497

Ribadeneyra, *Vida*, FN 4:260-263, 720-721, 924-925

Ad Simonem Rodericum socium morti proximum octodecim milliarium itinere, febri ipse
laborans propere contendit, eumq̄ amplexu sanat.

50

51

E sociis unus cum tentatione iam victus ad
solitudinem pergeret, obiecto sibi armati fer-
rumque intentantis equitis spectro, ad Ignatium
remittitur, qui re tota per prophetiae spiritum
cognita redeuntem illis Domini verbis blande
excipit: Modicae fidei quare dubitasti!

One of the companions,
overcome by temptation, sought solitude;
confronted by the spectre of a knight in armor brandishing a sword,
he is sent back to Ignatius,
who by a spirit of prophecy understands the whole matter
and gently welcomes him, as he returns, with the Lord's own words:
"O you of little faith, why did you doubt?" [Matt 14:31]

Ribadeneyra, *Vida*, FN 4:768-769

E socijs vnus, cum tentatione iam victus ad
solitudinem pergeret, obiecto sibi armati, fer-
rumq̃ intentantis equitis spectro, ad Ignatium
remittitur, qui re tota per prophetiæ spiritum
cognita, redeuntem, illis Domini verbis blande
excipit. Modicæ fidei quare dubitas ti!

53

52

Solitario homini eius vitam tacite despicienti
apparet Dominus, ac viri sanctitatem aperit do-
cetque illum ad salutem plurimorum natum esse.

There was a hermit who without saying so disdained his life:
the Lord appears to him, reveals the sanctity of the man,
and teaches him that Ignatius was born for the salvation of many.

Ribadeneyra, *Vida*, FN 4:262-263

Solitario homini eius vitam tacite despicienti
apparet Dominus, ac viri sanctitatem aperit, do-
cetq̃ illum ad salutem plurimorum natum esse.

52.

53

Non longe ab Urbe templum desertum ingresso
inter orandum se Deus Pater ostendens illum fi-
lio suo crucem gestanti socium attribuit; filius
item placidissima illa verba pronuntians EGO VO-
BIS ROMAE PROPITIUS ERO illum recipit in socium.
Unde Ignatio lux oborta societatis IESU nominandae.

Not far from Rome he entered a deserted church
and while he was praying God the Father shows Himself
and gives him as companion to His Son as He carries the cross.
Likewise, the Son, pronouncing those gentle words,
"I will be propitious to you in Rome," welcomes him as companion.
Thus the light dawned on Ignatius
to call the Society by the name of Jesus.

The famous vision took place at the little hamlet of La Storta on the outskirts of Rome.

Ignatius, *Acta* (#96), FN 1:496-499

Ribadeneyra, *Vida*, FN 4:268-275

Non longe ab Vrbe templum desertum ingresso
inter orandum se Deus Pater ostendens illum fi-
lio suo crucem gestanti socium attribuit; filius
item placidissima illa verba pronuntians EGO VO-
BIS ROMÆ PROPITIVS ERO illū recipit in socium
Vnde Ignatio lux oborta societatis IESV nominandæ.

53

54

Primum sacrum Romae ad Domini praesepe
facit, cum se ad id post susceptum sacerdotium
duodeviginti mensium studio praeparasset.

He offers his first Mass in Rome at the manger of the Lord;
he had earnestly prepared himself for it,
after being ordained priest, for eighteen months.

---

at the manger: i.e., in the church of St. Mary Major

Ignatius, Acta (#96), FN 1:496-499

Ribadeneyra, *Vida*, FN 4:268-269

Primum sacrum Romæ ad Domini præsepe
facit, cum se ad id post susceptum sacerdotium
duodeuiginti mensium studio præparasset.

54

55

In Casinati monte ut S. Benedictus Ger-
mani sic ille animam Hozij ferri in coelum
videt ac postea in ipso missae cui astabat
ingressu ad ea verba et omnibus sanctis in
illustri sanctorum choro socium agnoscit.

In Monte Cassino just as St. Benedict had a vision of Germanus,
so he sees the soul of Hoces being borne aloft to heaven,
and afterwards at the very beginning of a Mass he attended,
at the words "and to all the saints," in
the shining choir of saints he recognizes his companion.

St. Germanus of Capua (d. 545) was a great friend of St. Benedict, founder of the
Benedictines and of the monastery of Monte Cassino, located southeast of Rome. Diego de
Hoces (d. 1538), a priest from Málaga, joined Ignatius and his companions in Venice but died
in Padua before the founding of the Society.

Ignatius, *Acta* (#98), FN 1:500-503

Ribadeneyra, *Vida,* FN 4:276-279

In Casinati monte vt S. Benedictus Ger=
mani, sic ille animam Hozij ferri in coelum
videt, ac postea in ipso missæ, cui astabat
ingressu ad ea verba et omnibus sanctis in
illustri sanctorum choro socium agnoscit.

55

56

Paulus III Pont. Max. Societatis Iesu insti-
tutum ab Ignatio oblatum postquam legisset;
DIGITUS inquit DEI EST HIC Socie-
tatemque confirmat anno salutis 1540.

Paul III, Supreme Pontiff, having read
the [Formula of the] Institute of the Society of Jesus
proposed by Ignatius, says, "The finger of God is here,"
and confirms the Society in the year of salvation 1540.

Ribadeneyra, *Vida*, FN 4:308-311

Paulus III Pont. Max. Societatis Iesu insti=
tutum ab Ignatio oblatum postquam legisset,
DIGITVS, inquit, DEI EST HIC. Socie =
tatemque confirmat anno salutis 1540.

56

57

Franciscum Xaverium qui Indiarum
Apostolus dictus est divino instinctus
afflatu in Indias mittit.

Impelled by a divine inspiration,
he sends to the Indies Francis Xavier,
who has come to be called Apostle to the Indies.

Ribadeneyra, *Vida*, FN 4:302-303

Franciscum Xauerium, qui Indiarum
Apostolus dictus est, diuino instinctus
afflatu in Indias mittit.

57

58

Generalis quamquam invitus diuque repugnans
eligitur atque in aede quae extra urbem
visitur Sancti Pauli quarto solemni voto se
ac societatem suam Romano Pontifici obstringit.

Though unwilling and for a long time resisting,
he is elected General; and in the church of St. Paul,
which is visited outside the City, he binds himself and his society
by a solemn fourth vow to the Roman Pontiff.

Ribadeneyra, *Vida*, FN 4:368-373

Generalis quamquam inuitus, diuq́ repugnans,
eligitur ; atque in æde, quæ extra vrbem
visitur, Sancti Pauli quarto solemni voto se,
ac Societatem suam Romano Pontifici obstringit.

58

59

Ex l[itte]ris B. Xaverij ad Ignatium ex India scriptis:
GRATIA ET CARITAS X. D. etc. Mi pater in X^i. visceribus unice.
Te ego pater animae meae summeque mihi venerande positis humi ge-
nibus (sic n[unc] hanc tibi ep[istu]lam scribo) suppliciter oro ut mihi a
Deo impetres ut dum vivam sanctissimae voluntatis suae mihi det
et plane agnoscendae et omnino exequendae facultatem. Vale.
Tuus minimus filius longissimeque exulans.

FRANC^S XAVERIUS.

From the letters of Blessed Xavier to Ignatius, written from India:
May the grace and charity of Christ our Lord [be ever with us.
Amen.] My only father in Christi visceribus: I pray you, father of my
soul, revered by me in highest measure, kneeling upon the ground
(as I am now, writing this letter to you), that you implore God that
whilst I live he may give me to know clearly and to carry out
entirely his holy will. Farewell. Your least son, in distant exile.

Francis Xavier.

Letter written from Cochin, January 14, 1549. Slightly different version in M. Joseph
Costelloe, The Letters and Instructions of Francis Xavier (St. Louis, Missouri: Institute of
Jesuit Sources, 1992), p. 227. in Christi visceribus: lit., "in the bowels of Christ"; "bowels" is the
older rendering (as in the Douay-Rheims and King James versions) for the scriptural
expression now translated as "mercy" or "compassion"; cf., e.g., Phil 1:8.

Ribadeneyra, *Vida*, FN 4:722-723

Ex lris B.Xauerij, ad Ignatium ex India scriptis
GRATIA ET CARITAS X.¹ D. &c. Mi pater in X.¹ viſceriḃ vnice
Te ego pater animæ meæ, ſumeĝ mihi venerande poſitis humi ge﹕
nibus (ſic.n.hanc tibi eptam ſcribo) ſuppliciter oro, vt mihi a
Deo impetres, vt dum viuam ſanctiſſimæ voluntatis ſuæ mihi det
et plane agnoſcendæ, et omnino exequendæ facultatem. Vale
Tuus minimus filius, longiſſimeĝ exulans. FRANC.XAVERIVS. 59

60

Sacramentorum piarumque concionum usum Romae
renovat ac rationem pueris tradendi doctrinae
christianae rudimenta Romanis in templis
ac plateis inducit.

In Rome, he renews the practice of frequenting the sacraments
and of giving devout sermons and introduces ways of passing
on the rudiments of Christian doctrine to youth
in the churches and squares of Rome.

Ignatius, *Acta* (#98), FN 1:500-503

Ribadeneyra, *Vida,* FN 4:374-375

Sacramentorum ,piarumq̃ concionum v∫ũ Romæ
renouat, ac rationem pueris tradendi doctrinæ
christianæ rudimenta Romanis in templis,
ac plateis inducit.

60

61

Dum Romae insimulatur quod multorum
scelerum diversis in urbibus damnatus
fuisset, divina providentia Romam simul
confluunt omnes qui illum alibi absolverant,
ijdem eius innocentiae antea iudices nunc testes.

When at Rome the charge is brought that he had been
condemned of many crimes in various cities,
by divine providence there stream together into Rome persons
who elsewhere had found him innocent;
and those who formerly were his judges
now are witnesses to his innocence.

Ignatius, *Acta* (#98), FN 1:500-503
Ribadeneyra, *Vida*, FN 4:284-295

Dum Romæ, insimulatur, quod multorum
scelerum diuersis in Vrbibus damnatus
fuisset, diuina prouidentia Romam simul
confluunt omnes, qui illum alibi absoluerant,
ijdem eius innocentiæ antea iudices; nunc testes.

61

62

Ad aedem S. Petri in monte aureo contendens
rem sacram pro salute Codurij facturus, in medio
Sixti Ponte resistit continuo, coelumque tantisper
intuitus ac divinitus de eius morte admonitus,
Redeamus, inquit, socius mortuus est.

Hastening to the shrine of San Pietro in Montorio,
about to celebrate Mass for Codure's recovery,
he suddenly halts in the middle of the Ponte Sisto,
meanwhile looking at heaven, and by divine revelation
apprised of his death he says,
"Let us return: our companion has died."

Jean Codure was among the companions of Paris and therefore a founder of the Society. He died on August 29, 1541. Ignatius' companion on the way to San Pietro in Montorio, a small chapel designed by Bramante at the base of the Janiculum hill, was Giovanni Battista Viola.

Ribadeneyra, *Vida*, FN 4:370-373

Ad ædem S. Petri in monte aureo contendens,
rem sacram pro salute Codurij facturus, in medio
Sixti Ponte resistit continuo, coelumq̄ tantisper
intuitus, ac diuinitus de eius morte admonitus,
Redeamus, inquit, socius mortuus est.

63

Publica Romae pietatis opera instituit: coenobia mulie-
rum male nuptarum, virginum S. Catherinae ad funa-
rios puellarum SS. quatuor coronatorum; puerorum item
qui orbi parentibus per Urbem vagi mendicant; cathecume-
norum aliorumque collegia magna o[mn]ium admiratione fructuque.

At Rome he founds public works of piety:
hospices for women in bad marriages;
for virgins at [the church of] Santa Caterina dei Funari,
for [orphan] girls at [the church of] Santi Quattro Coronati,
also for orphan boys wandering through the city as beggars,
a residence for [Jewish] catechumens, as well as other residences
and colleges, to the profit and with the admiration of everybody.

Ignatius, *Acta* (#98), FN 1:500-503

Ribadeneyra, *Vida*, FN 4:402-415

Publica Romæ pietatis opera instituit: coenobia mlie-
rum male nuptarum: virginum S. Catherinæ ad funa-
rios: puellarum SS. quatuor coronatorum: puerorũ item
qui orbi parentibus per Vrbem vagi mendicant: Cathecume-
norum: aliorumq̃ Collegia magna oĩum admiratione, fructuq̃.

63

64

Ignatij in Septemtrionis res apprime intenti
studio ac precibus Iulius III Pont.Max. Collegium
Germaniae iuventutis non minori Ecclesiae Romanae
ornamento quam Germanicae praesidio Romae condit.

Because of Ignatius's special interest
in Northern European matters and his entreaties,
Julius III, Supreme Pontiff,
founds a college in Rome for the youth of Germany,
no less as an ornament of the Roman Church
than as a bulwark for Germany.

This is the German College, founded in 1552 and still operating today.
Ribadeneyra, *Vida*, FN 4:630-637

Ignatij in *Septemtrionis* res apprime intenti
studio, ac precibus Iulius III. Pont. Max. Collegium
Germaniæ iuuentutis non minori Ecclesiæ Romanæ
ornamento, quam Germaniæ præsidio Romæ condit.

64

65

*Societatis Iesu constitutiones frequentibus
sanctissimae Trinitatis apparitionibus atque
illustrationibus, Beatissima item virgine saepe visa, atque illas approbante conscribit.*

With frequent manifestations and illuminations
of the Most Holy Trinity and the Blessed Virgin,
appearing and bestowing approval on them,
he writes the Constitutions of the Society of Jesus.

Ignatius, *Acta* (#100), FN 1:504-507

Ribadeneyra, *Vida*, FN 4:610-615

Societatis Iesu constitutiones frequentibus
sanctissimæ Trinitatis apparitionibus, atque
illustrationibus. Beatissima item virgine sæpe visa, atq; illas approbante conscribit.

65.

66

Obstinatum Iudaeum tribus hisce verbis
convertit: Mane nobiscum Isaac.

With these three words he converts a determined Jew:
"Stay with us, Isaac."

Mane nobiscum: Luke 24:29

Ribadeneyra, *Vida,* FN 4:816-817

Obstinatum Iudæum tribus hisce verbis
conuertit. MANE NOBISCVM ISAAC.

66

67

Saepe noctu inter orandum aut qui-
escendum a Daemonibus verberatur.

Often at night while at prayer or at rest
he is beaten by demons.

Ribadeneyra, *Vida*, FN 4:848-849

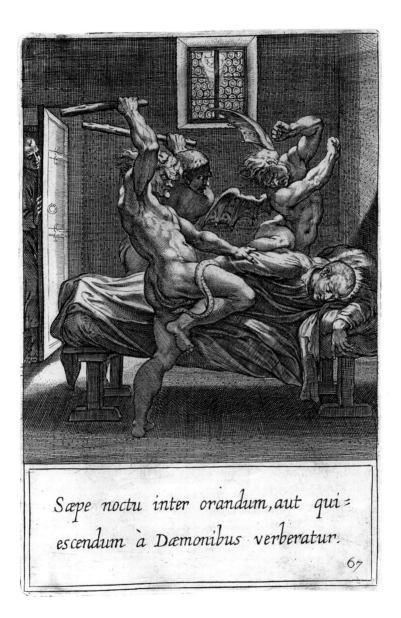

Sæpe noctu inter orandum, aut qui=
escendum à Dæmonibus verberatur.

67

68

Caeli aspectu mirifice captus vim lacrymarum
profundere atque exclamare solebat, HEU QUAM
SORDET TELLUS CUM COELUM ASPICIO, *cumque prae*
lacrymis oculos perderet, imperium in illas a Deo
impetrat; novoque dono donum lacrymarum moderatur.

Caught up in marvelous wise by the sight of the heavens,
he was accustomed to shed forceful tears and to exclaim,
"ALAS, HOW BASE IS EARTH WHEN I BEHOLD HEAVEN";
and when because of the tears he might lose his sight
he begs God for control of them,
and by a new gift the gift of tears is abated.

Ribadeneyra, *Vida*, FN 4:94-95

Caeli aspectu mirifice captus vim lacrymarum
profundere, atq; exclamare solebat, HEV QVAM
SORDET TELLVS, CVM COELVM ASPICIO? cumq; præ
lacrymis oculos perderet, imperium in illas à Deo
impetrat; nouoq; dono donum lacrymarũ moderatur.

68

69

Sacram hostiam Deo dum offert supra
missam celebrantis caput, ingens emicare
flamma conspicitur.

When he offers the sacred Host to God
as he celebrates Mass,
a huge flame is seen to break forth above his head.

Sacram hostiam Deo dum offert, supra
missam celebrantis caput, ingens emicare
flamma conspicitur.

69

70

Allatum e patria fasciculum litterarum
redditumque inter orandum, in proximum ignem
abjicit: curasque saeculi importune interpellantes
una cum litteris concremandas dedit.

A bundle of letters brought from his native land,
and handed to him while at prayer, he throws into the nearby fire;
and concerns of the world inconveniently interrupting him
he consigns to be burnt together with the letters.

Allatum e patria fasciculum litterarum,
redditumq̃ inter orandum, in proximum ignem
abijcit: curasq̃ sæculi importune interpellantes
vna cum litteris concremandas dedit.

70

71

Prophetiae sp[irit]u videt arcana animorum
ac saepe futura praesentit, inter alia
aegrotanti praedicit aspectu illum Virginis
fruiturum, dictisque consentit eventus.

By the spirit of prophecy he sees things hidden within souls
and often knows things that are to be;
among other things he predicts to a sick person
that he is to enjoy the face of the Virgin,
and the outcome matches what he said.

Prophetiæ s̄pu videt arcana animorum,
ac sæpe futura præsentit; inter alia
ægrotanti prædicit, aspectu illum Virginis
fruiturum, dictisque consentit euentus.

72

*Daemonem serpentis facie collucentis
exhibentem se tetegit, ac per contemptum
baculo abigit.*

A demon with the face of a shining serpent
shows itself and he unmasks it
and contemptuously drives it away with a staff.

Ignatius, *Acta* (#31), FN 1:406-407

Dæmonem serpentis facie collucentis
exhibentem se detegit, ac per contemptum
baculo abigit

72

73

Saepe B. Philippus Nerius illius faciem
insigni luce radiantem videt illustri,
ut ipse dicebat, indicio sanctitatis.

Often Blessed Philip Neri sees his face
glowing with a remarkable light—
as he would say, a clear indication of sanctity.

Saint Philip Neri, founder of the Oratorians and younger contemporary of Ignatius, lived in
Rome at the same time as Ignatius.

Ribadeneyra, *Flos sanctorum,* 2:843

Sæpe B. Philippus Nerius illius faciem
insigni luce radiantem videt, illuſtri,
vt ipse dicebat, indicio sanctitatis.

73

74

Alexandri Petronii morbo laborantis cu-
biculum adventu suo, magno repente
fulgore collustrat aegrum, colloquio sanat,
ac saepe alios invisens itidem sanat.

By his arrival, suddenly with great thunder
he brightens the room of Alexander Petronius,
suffering from illness; heals the sick man with his conversation,
and often in the same way, by visiting them, heals others.

Ribadeneyra, *Flos sanctorum*, 2:843. According to Ribadeneyra, Petronius was a much respected medical doctor in Rome who was a friend of Ignatius.

Alexandri Petronij morbo laborantis cu=
biculum aduentu suo, magno repente
fulgore collustrat: ægrum colloquio sanat;
ac sæpe alios inuisens itidem sanat.

74

75

Patres Collegii Lauretani cum Lemurum
spectris infestarentur, ad eius preces
per litteras confugiunt; eiusque accepto
responso ac publice perlecto, illico Dae-
monum terroribus liberantur.

Fathers of the College of Loreto,
when they had an infestation of ghostly spectres,
have recourse by letter to his prayers;
and when his reply comes and is read in public,
on the spot they are freed from the terrors of the demons.

The school at Loreto, location of the famous shrine of the Holy House of Nazareth, was among the first founded by the Jesuits.

Ribadeneyra, *Flos sanctorum*, 2:848

Patres Collegij Lauretani, cum Lemurum
spectris infestarentur, ad eius preces
per litteras confugiunt; eiusque accepto
responso, ac publice perlecto, illico Dæ-
monum terroribus liberantur.

75

76

Cuidam e Societate Romam venire
Colonia meditanti, ut illius aspectu frue-
retur, ultro ipse apparet seque Coloniae
videndum socio praebet.

To a certain man of the Society who was thinking
of coming to Rome from Cologne
so that he might have the satisfaction of seeing Ignatius's face,
he himself spontaneously appears and presents himself
to the companion to be seen in Cologne.

The Jesuit was Leonard Kessel, one of the first Germans to enter the Society.

Ribadeneyra, *Flos sanctorum,* 2:842

Cuidam e Societate Romam venire,
Colonia meditanti, vt illius aspectu frue:
retur, vltro ipse apparet, seque Coloniæ
videndum socio præbet.

76

Romae sanctissime moritur eodemque
puncto temporis beata eius anima ingenti
splendore conspicua, Bononiae a nobili
sanctaque foemina ferri in coelum aspicitur.

At Rome he dies a most holy death,
and at that very moment his blessed soul,
outstanding for great splendor,
is seen at Bologna by a noble and holy woman,
as it is borne to heaven.

Ribadeneyra, *Vida*, FN 4:708-713

Romæ sanctissime moritur, eodemque
puncto temporis beata eius anima, ingenti
splendore conspicua, Bononiæ a nobili,
sanctaq̃ foemina ferri in coelum aspicitur.

77

78

Puella strumis iam diu laborans cum
ad manus iacentis in pheretro deosculan-
das accedere prae turba non posset, frustato
vestis arrepto et ad collum alligato illico
sanatur: folia passim ac flores e pheretro
subducti aegrorum multis saluti sunt.

A girl afflicted for a long time with a tumor,
who because of the throng could not get close to him
to kiss his hands as he lay on the bier,
with a piece of cloth torn from his garment
and applied to her neck is healed on the spot.
Leaves and flowers taken from the bier
help the healing of sick people far and wide.

Reminiscences of Matt 9:20-22; Mark 2:4, prae turba
Ribadeneyra, *Flos sanctorum*, 2:855-856

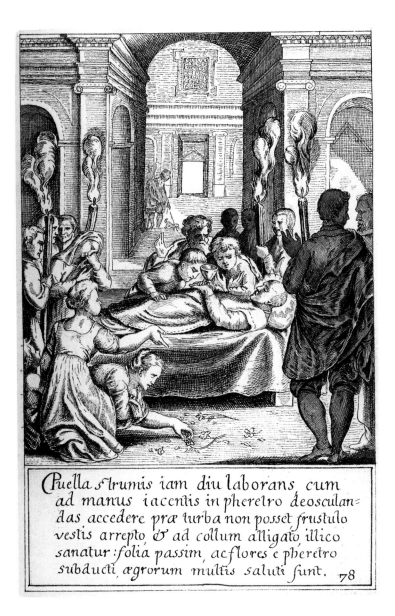

Puella strumis iam diu laborans, cum
ad manus iacentis in pheretro deosculan=
das accedere præ turba non posset frustulo
vestis arrepto, & ad collum alligato illico
sanatur : folia passim, ac flores e pheretro
subducti, ægrorum multis saluti sunt. 78

79

Dum eius transferuntur sacra ossa
lucentes stellae in loculo visae, ac
caelestis inibi concentus auditus.

As his holy bones are translated,
shining stars appear in the burial place,
and heavenly singing is heard there too.

Ribadeneyra, *Flos sanctorum*, 2:856

Dum eius transferuntur sacra ossa,
lucentes stellæ in loculo visæ, ac
caelestis inibi concentus auditus.

79